Here are the amazing stories behind the food and products millions of people consume and use every day. Birdseye, Hershey, Wrigley, Buick, Goodyear, Kellogg, Kraft, Woolworth ... these are just a few of the real people you will meet in this book whose names have become household words. Whether they were motivated by necessity or curiosity, or just stumbled upon their inventions by accident, these fascinating entrepreneurs have truly left their brands on America!

INVENTORS WHO LEFT THEIR
BRANDS
ON AMERICA

Frank H. Olsen

BANTAM BOOKS

NEW YORK · TORONTO · LONDON · SYDNEY · AUCKLAND

RL 5, age 10 and up

INVENTORS WHO LEFT THEIR BRANDS ON AMERICA
A Bantam Book/October 1991

Photo Credits

1. Photo courtesy of the Firestone Tire & Rubber Co. 2. Photo courtesy of Frito-Lay®, Inc. 3. Photo courtesy of Parker Brothers 4. Photo courtesy of Hewlett-Packard Company 5. Photo courtesy of Wm. Wrigley Jr. Company 6. Photo reprinted courtesy of Eastman Kodak Company 7. Photo courtesy of the Rowland Institute for Science 8. Photo courtesy of Gerber Products Company 9. Photo courtesy of the Gillette Company 10. Photograph courtesy of the Fuller Brush Company, Great Bend, Kansas 11. Photo courtesy of Woolworth Corporation, New York 12. Photo courtesy of Otis Elevator Company 13. Photo courtesy of the Famous Amos Chocolate Chip Cookie Corporation 14. Photo courtesy of Elizabeth Arden Archives 15. Photo courtesy of Mary Kay Cosmetics, Inc. 16. Photo courtesy of Borden, Inc. 17. Photo courtesy of Sears, Roebuck and Co. 18. Photo courtesy of Baldwin Piano and Organ Company 19. Photo courtesy of Kentucky Fried Chicken 20. Photo courtesy of Reynolds Metals Company 21. Photo courtesy of The Proctor & Gamble Company 22. Photo courtesy of Ford Motor Company 23. Photo courtesy of H. J. Heinz Company 24. Photo reproduced with permission of Kraft General Foods, Inc. 25. Photo courtesy of J. C. Penney Company, Inc.

Bantam Books are published by Bantam Books, a division of Bantam Doubleday Dell Publishing Group, Inc. Its trademark, consisting of the words "Bantam Books" and the portrayal of a rooster, is Registered in U.S. Patent and Trademark Office and in other countries. Marca Registrada. Bantam Books, 666 Fifth Avenue, New York, New York 10103.

PRINTED IN THE UNITED STATES OF AMERICA

RAD 0 9 8 7 6 5 4 3 2 1

Contents

Introduction

Levi's, Birdseye, Borden, Hershey, Wrigley's, McDonald's—just say the brand name and the person to whom you're speaking will immediately know the corresponding product. But few people realize that these are the names of real people—inventors, merchants, and entrepreneurs—who, for a variety of reasons, created the products. Many struggled against great odds and frequent failures before their dreams became reality, and their stories are awesome and inspiring.

Most of the enterprising people of the nineteenth and early twentieth centuries were European immigrants; very few women or African Americans were given opportunities to make significant contributions in areas of invention and business. Fortunately, society has changed, and today men and women of all races, ethnicities, and religions become successful inventors and entrepreneurs.

In the nineteenth century, most goods were made locally and sold in bulk. You could walk into any grocery store and find open barrels of crackers; sacks of flour, cornmeal, and coffee beans; and large metal cans of milk. Dry products were weighed in the store and packaged in paper, and customers had to bring their own jugs to be filled with milk.

It wasn't until the late 1800s that merchandise produced in factories and sold in packages began to replace locally produced goods, and with this change came the widespread use of trademarks and brand names. The concept of trademarks was actually introduced as early as 1266 when an English law was passed requiring bakers to put their mark on every loaf of bread. If a loaf was found to be underweight the mark would identify the baker. Goldsmiths and silversmiths were also required to place a personal symbol on every piece they made as a guarantee that the metal was of the highest quality. Today, almost everything we purchase is individually packaged and identified by a brand name.

Many of the fascinating people you will meet in this book were pioneers. Some started inventing at an early age, and many began their businesses with very little money. In some cases it was a matter of being in the right place at the right time that accounted for a successful invention; others stumbled upon their inventions by accident. Some people had a need for a particular device or product and decided to make it themselves. Others took an already existing product and made it better. But no matter what the means or situation, most of the inventors had one thing in common—they believed in themselves and they were determined to succeed. These people have left their brands on America.

★ 1 ★

Never Too Young

Thomas Edison was only twelve years old when he began the experiments that would one day make him one of the most productive and best-known inventors in the world. His early start was by no means unique.

At the end of the nineteenth century and during the early years of this century, there were many individuals who were known as *tinkerers*. It was the beginning of the industrial age, when newer and better products were waiting to be invented, and even if the tinkerers had little formal education, they had inventive minds and curious imaginations.

★ S. Duncan Black and Alonzo G. Decker
(Black & Decker Tools)

There are some names that just seem to go together, like two interlocking pieces of a jigsaw puzzle. What would Procter be without Gamble? Or Sears without Roebuck? Each pair has become linked for all time in the minds of consumers everywhere. Black and Decker are two names that fit together as smoothly as the interlocking joints that their power tools make possible.

Duncan Black and Alonzo Decker became good friends when they worked for the Rowland Telegraph Company in Baltimore, Maryland. With a common interest in mechanics, they decided to quit their jobs and go into business for themselves as designers and manufacturers of industrial machinery and tools.

Launching a new business, of course, required start-up money. Decker sold the one thing he prized the most—a 1907 Maxwell automobile—for six hundred dollars. Black borrowed the same amount of money from his father-in-law.

Still in their twenties, the two young men opened their first plant in downtown Baltimore. The year was 1910. It wasn't long before they had designed and built a machine for putting caps on milk bottles, a candy dipper, a postage stamp slitter, a cotton picker, a shock absorber for the automobile industry, and various machinery for the United States Mint.

In 1914, Black and Decker produced the

world's first electric drill. This innovation was what industry had been waiting for. Within ten years, the two young men had turned their original twelve-hundred-dollar investment into annual sales of over one million dollars. It wasn't until 1946, however, that Black and Decker introduced their first line of drills and accessories for the home market. Their timing was perfect.

World War II had just ended and returning veterans were buying homes and getting into home building projects. The "do-it-yourself" fad was here to stay—and so was Black and Decker.

★ David L. Clark
(Clark Bar)

David Clark came to America from Ireland. While still a teenager, he began making candy in the back of a small house in Pittsburgh. It wasn't long before his chocolate drops and other "penny candy" items became very popular in the local area. By the time the United States entered World War I in 1917, Clark's reputation had come to the attention of the U.S. Army, which contracted with him to supply candy to American soldiers overseas. The boys in uniform liked the chocolate treats, though there was a problem.

Until that time, most candy was unwrapped and sold "loose" in open dishes or cardboard trays on store counters and shelves. Clark shipped his candy to the stores in thirty-pound cases, but these were too bulky for the Army to carry on the battlefields. The Pennsylvania candymaker came up with a practical solution. He began to manufacture his popular chocolates in small bars and wrap them individually; hence the *Clark Bar* was born.

The self-made millionaire, who had come to these shores as a penniless immigrant, later added chewing gum to his line of confections. *Clark's Teaberry Gum* is still sold today.

David Clark continued to run his candy empire until his death in 1939 at the age of seventy-five.

★ Thomas Alva Edison

Much has been written about Thomas Edison and his numerous inventions that have so drastically changed the way we live today. What is not widely known is that this electrical and mechanical genius dropped out of school. At age twelve, he began working as a newsboy on the Grand Trunk Railway and devoted his spare time to experiments in a laboratory he had set up in a freight car.

One day, young Edison saved the life of the stationmaster's child by pulling him out of the way of an approaching boxcar. He was rewarded by being taught telegraphy. Although Edison became an excellent telegraph operator, he was more interested in his experiments and was never able to hold on to a job for any length of time. It was while he was working as a telegraph operator, however, that he came up with his first important invention—an instrument that enabled messages to be repeated automatically without an operator.

Years later, after making many improvements to the system, Edison began selling telegraphic appliances. With the forty thousand dollars he earned, he opened his own laboratory in 1876. The next year, Edison announced his invention of a phonograph that could record sound mechanically on a tinfoil-wrapped cylinder. Two years later, he displayed his most important invention—the incandescent electric light bulb.

★ Harvey S. Firestone
(Firestone Tire & Rubber Co.)

Harvey Firestone was born on his father's farm in Columbiana, Ohio, in 1868. The short and slender youth studied briefly at a business college in Cleveland, worked for a while as a bookkeeper, and then sold patent medicine. In 1890, at the age of twenty-two, he thought it was time to settle down so he took a job with the Columbus Buggy Company, owned by his uncle. Firestone discovered that he was a born salesman and did very well, but his career ended abruptly when the company went bankrupt in 1896.

While Firestone worked for his uncle, he foresaw that the iron-banded wheels used on most buggies would soon be replaced by rubber tires that would make travel less bumpy. He talked a friend into investing money in a rubber manufacturing business, and at twenty-seven, the emerging entrepreneur became president of the Firestone Rubber Company in Chicago. Four years later, he sold his share of the business at a tremendous profit and moved his family to Akron, Ohio, which had already become the rubber capital of the world. In 1900, Harvey Firestone hired seventeen workers and formed the Firestone Tire and Rubber Company. It wasn't long before his company was supplying the growing automobile industry with solid rubber and pneumatic tires.

In 1906, Firestone's fortune took an upward turn when Henry Ford selected Firestone tires for his automobiles. The two industrialists were to become close friends for the remainder of their lives, and their two companies would become leaders in the automotive world.

In 1923, Firestone introduced the balloon tire, which many car manufacturers quickly adopted as standard equipment. To encourage automobile travel, Firestone pioneered one-stop service stations where motorists could buy gas, oil, and, of course, Firestone tires.

In the early 1900s, most of the rubber plantations were controlled by the British. When the British decided to curtail the output from these plantations in order to raise the price of crude rubber, Firestone leased a million acres in Liberia and developed his own plantations. This turned out to be a valuable source of rubber for the Allies during World War II. Harvey Firestone's investment in Liberia played an influential role in developing the economy of the African nation.

★ Herman W. Lay
(Lay's® Brand Potato Chips)

Americans eat more potato chips than any other people in the world. But it wasn't always so. In fact, potato chips did not originate until 1853 when a customer in an elegant New York State resort complained about the fried potatoes he was eating and the chef got angry enough to do something drastic.

The complaining diner was Cornelius Vanderbilt, known as "Commodore," the railroad and shipping tycoon. The chef was a Native American named George Crum. The Commodore sent the potatoes back to the kitchen with the curt comment, "Too thick." The cook was so offended by Vanderbilt's arrogant attitude that he cut a potato into paper-thin slices and fried them in hot oil until they were crisp. Much to his surprise, the Commodore liked these crunchy potato slices, and so did the friends at his table. Word soon spread about these "chips" and they become very popular in many Northern states. Potato chips didn't became a national snack food, however, until Herman W. Lay came upon the scene many years later.

Lay was born in Greenville, South Carolina,

in 1909. By the time he was old enough to work, the country was in the grips of the Great Depression. The young twenty-year-old sold jewelry in Greenville, then worked as a lumberjack and a wheat harvester in Washington.

Three years later, in 1932, he signed up as a potato chip salesman with the Barrett Food Products Company of Atlanta. He became a familiar sight to grocers in Nashville, Tennessee, as he drove up and down the streets and country roads, selling chips from the back of his Model A Ford. Before the year was out, Lay had borrowed one hundred dollars and bought the Barrett warehouse in Nashville.

By the time Herman Lay was twenty-five, he had six sales routes and was continually expanding his business. But in 1938, he got the bad news that his Atlanta supplier was having financial troubles and might have to close down. Acting quickly, the young businessman bought the company, moved to Atlanta, and became president of the newly named H. W. Lay Company—all before he turned thirty.

In 1945, Herman Lay joined forces with Elmer Doolin, who had started making Fritos in San Antonio, Texas, and the snack food giant, Frito-Lay®, was born.

★ George Swinnerton Parker
(Parker Brothers Games)

Most people like to play board games, and George Parker was no exception. But there were not that many board games on the market back in the early 1880s, so the creative youngster from Medford, Massachusetts, decided to create his own. He invented his first game when he was only sixteen. It was obvious that Parker had his mind set on making money, because he called his creation *Banking*.

The enterprising young man persuaded his high school principal to give him a three-week leave of absence so he could produce and sell five hundred copies of the game in time for the upcoming Christmas season.

Despite the success of his first venture, Parker's parents were not impressed and encouraged their son to forget game making and take up the more secure business of journalism. To please his parents, Parker accepted a job as a cub reporter for a Boston newspaper after high school graduation. But a repiratory ailment soon made it necessary for him to find a less strenuous job. This gave him the excuse to go back to what he really wanted to do—create games. He teamed up with his brother Charles and formed the Parker Brothers game company in 1896. A third brother, Edward, joined the business two years later.

The game that made the company world famous—*Monopoly*—was not invented by George and almost did not become a Parker Brothers product.

During the early days of the Depression, an unemployed engineer named Charles Darrow spent hours at his Germantown, Pennsylvania, home devising new board games to keep his mind off his poverty. Since money was so scarce, he decided that what Americans needed was a game in which they could buy and sell real estate for large sums of "cash."

Darrow thought back to the carefree days when he used to spend vacations in Atlantic City, New Jersey. The streets of his favorite resort city became the squares on the board, and obtaining choice real estate along the boardwalk became the goal of the game.

Darrow was persuaded by friends to sell his creation to Parker Brothers. Company officials test-played the game and said that it was dull, slow moving, and very complicated to play. Disappointed but undaunted, Darrow found an executive at Wanamaker's department store in Philadelphia who enjoyed playing the game and wanted to put it on sale in his store. With money borrowed from family and friends, the creator of Monopoly had five thousand games manufactured and delivered to Wanamaker's. The game proved an instant success and sold out almost immediately. When news of this reached Parker Brothers, they took another look at the game and decided that it was "imaginative, fast-paced, and easy to learn."

Parker Brothers soon found themselves with a "monopoly" on their hands as the board game

outsold all others on the market. The Massachusetts firm was turning out twenty thousand Monopoly sets a week. Today, more than fifty-five
years later, Monopoly is one of the two longest
selling and best-selling board games of this century. The other game is Scrabble.

★ 2 ★
Modest Beginnings

If it is true that some of the largest trees in the forest started out as tiny seeds, then it should not be surprising that some of today's biggest corporations began with investments as small as a few hundred dollars. These modest beginnings, in most cases, represented the entire life savings of the entrepreneurs. These business pioneers were willing to risk everything they had for a dream and a chance for success. The beginnings may have been modest but the visions were not.

★ Thomas Armstrong
(Armstrong Floors and Ceilings)

In 1860, the same year that a British inventor named Frederick Walton received a patent for a hard, shiny floor covering called *linoleum*, an American named Thomas Armstrong bought a machine to cut cork into bottle stoppers. Although unrelated, the two events would soon come together into a successful business that today is a leader in floor coverings and ceiling tiles.

Thomas Morton Armstrong was an industrious twenty-four-year-old who was looking for a way to supplement his small income as a shipping clerk in a Pittsburgh glass plant. The bottles that his company made used cork stoppers. The bottles were reusable, but the corks were always thrown away. Seeing a need for a continuous supply of the cork plugs, Armstrong took his entire savings of three hundred dollars and started his own business.

He was just beginning to make a small profit when the Civil War broke out a year later. Armstrong was one of several businessmen who were asked to make medical supplies for the Union troops. True to his ethical standards, he was the only supplier who did not substitute inferior materials in order to make a bigger profit. When the frauds came to light, the young cork manufacturer was widely hailed for his honesty.

The publicity he received brought an avalanche of orders, and his company soon became a leader in the cork industry. Then came the invention of the screw-top bottle cap, and Armstrong knew he had to find other uses for cork.

It was then that he heard of a popular new floor covering—linoleum—that was made from cork dust and often backed with sheets of cork. Armstrong knew he had found the answer. In 1908, he began selling "linoleum carpet" in a variety of colors and patterns. His advertisements caught the eye of every American housewife who wanted to "beautify the home" and make it easier to keep clean at the same time.

Armstrong was one of the first manufacturers to put his name on his linoleum floor coverings, and he guaranteed everything he sold. His products could be shipped anywhere in the country, and customers trusted them because of the company's outstanding reputation.

Before the turn of the century, many businesses in America followed the ancient rule of *caveat emptor*: "Let the buyer beware." Armstrong's guiding principle was "Let the buyer have faith."

★ Walt Disney
(Walt Disney Productions)

It seems that Walt Disney was a success at everything he tried—movies, television, books, and amusement parks—but it wasn't always that way. He grew up on a small farm in Missouri, and dropped out of school at sixteen. After moving to Chicago, he struggled in such low-paying jobs as paper boy, mail sorter, and ambulance driver. He studied for a short time at an art school in Chicago, then moved back to Missouri, where he enrolled in another art school in Kansas City.

While barely into his twenties, Walt Disney opened his first cartoon business in Kansas City, but it soon went bankrupt. In 1923, the twenty-two-year-old arrived in Hollywood with only forty dollars in his pocket.

His brother, Roy, was already in Hollywood, turning out silent movies in a garage. Walt joined his brother, hired a couple of artists, and started producing animated motion pictures in the same garage.

Disney was beginning to attract some attention with his black-and-white cartoons, but his big moment came in 1928 when he released an animated cartoon called "Steamboat Willie." The short film featured a mouse named Mickey.

For most of his life, Walt Disney was the voice of Mickey Mouse. Ironically, the famous cartoon maker was not able to draw any of his famous characters. They were all produced by a staff of animators, and he asked his artists to show him how to turn out quick sketches of Mickey to include with his autographs.

Walt Disney may not have been a great cartoonist, but he was a genius at coming up with ideas and stories. Many years after his death, he is still drawing millions to Walt Disney World and Disneyland.

★ William Hewlett and David Packard
(Hewlett-Packard Computers)

The name Hewlett-Packard means high technology. The company has been making computers, calculators, and scientific instruments for many years. In fact, Hewlett-Packard was one of the first electronic companies to set up shop in what is now known as Silicon Valley, just south of San Francisco.

William Hewlett and David Packard were engineering classmates at Stanford University in California. Six-foot-five David played football and basketball, while William spent most of his time experimenting in the laboratory. But the sports jock also had a keen business mind, so after graduation the two pooled their total assets of $595 and started a company in a one-car garage in Palo Alto.

It was in another Palo Alto garage, twenty-six years earlier, that Lee DeForest had developed the three-electrode vacuum tube that would make radio, television, and computers possible. William Hewlett may have remembered that bit of history when he invented a new type of audio oscillator, an instrument for measuring sound waves. The first big order came from Walt Disney Studios which bought eight of the oscillators to help create the complex sound system for the movie *Fantasia*.

During World War II, Hewlett and Packard were asked by the government to build microwave signal generators. After the war, the electronics business started to boom, and Hewlett-Packard was ready. The company was soon turning out as many as two dozen new products a year. By the mid-1980s, Hewlett-Packard had become a world leader with annual sales of six billion dollars.

The company's philosophy has not changed since those days in that one-car garage. The key to success, Dave Packard believed, was good management, high technology, and a dedication to excellence.

★ Howard Johnson
(Howard Johnson's Ice Cream)

Howard Johnson loved ice cream. It was his favorite food from the time he was a young boy in Boston, Massachusetts. "When I dated the girl I later married," he said in later years, "we would drive fifteen miles to a certain place that had good ice cream."

It is not surprising, therefore, that Howard Johnson would later become known from coast to coast for his twenty-eight flavors of ice cream. His father, however, wondered if his only son would ever amount to anything.

When Howard was only five years old, his father put boxing gloves on the young boy to teach him the "manly art of boxing." When the elder Mr. Johnson threw an adult punch at his son's face, Howard ran crying to his mother with a bloody nose. "No whimpering, now," his father said. "I won't have him whimpering."

Although Howard's father was a harsh disciplinarian, he could also show love. When Mr. Johnson gave him a Shetland pony, Howard became the envy of all his friends. The future businessman made good use of the horse. Whenever he got tired during his paper route, or didn't feel like hoeing the vegetable garden, Howard could always find someone who would be willing to finish the job for him in exchange for a ride on the pony.

Despite Howard's cunning, his father instilled within him the value of hard work and an aggressive spirit. This was to pay off when his father died shortly after Howard returned home from France after World War I. Only then did he learn that the family cigar store business was $18,000 in debt. Howard ran the business for another three years, and managed to pay off eight thousand dollars of the debt. He then sold the business and took out personal loans for the $10,000 he still owed.

At the same time, the owner of a run-down store near the railroad station in Wollaston, a suburb of Boston, died leaving twenty-eight thousand dollars in debt. The relative who inherited the business came to Howard and begged him to take over the store and its debt. The sole heir offered to put up two thousand dollars in working capital if Howard could scrape up five hundred dollars. Although his friends thought he was foolish to do it, Howard managed to get the money and became the owner of a new business.

At the age of twenty-seven, Howard Johnson was forty thousand dollars in debt.

The store was called a drugstore, but no drugs were sold. There was a soda fountain, a candy and tobacco counter, and a newspaper stand. The first thing the young entrepreneur did was hire seventy-five boys and offer a home delivery service for the newspapers he sold. This became so popular with the citizens of Wollaston that the newspaper business alone was soon bringing in thirty thousand dollars a year.

Johnson next turned his attention to the soda fountain. Now he had a chance to make some money on the product he loved so much. The store only sold the standard three flavors— vanilla, chocolate, and strawberry—and they were just like all the other commercial brands. What Howard Johnson needed was an ice cream so good that people would come from all around to buy it.

There was such a product available. It was rich and creamy and sold from a pushcart by an old German peddler. With a little persuasion, Howard bought the recipe for only three hundred dollars.

The peddler's secret was doubling the butterfat content of commercial ice cream and using only natural flavorings. Johnson started making the ice cream in the basement of the store and the news soon spread throughout the neighborhood and the city.

When summer came, Johnson opened several ice cream stands at Boston beaches. By 1928, his ice cream sales had reached $240,000. He continued to experiment with new flavors and added them to the list. When he had reached twenty-eight flavors, he began to advertise, and the twenty-eight flavors remained a trademark for decades.

In 1929, Howard Johnson expanded into the restaurant business and almost lost all his money. He knew nothing about the business and had to learn as he went along. But learn he did, and by 1935, he had twenty-five restaurants alongside Massachusetts highways.

A yacht captain who owned a good location on Cape Cod tried to interest Johnson in leasing it for another restaurant. Johnson was still in debt, but the offer gave him an idea that was to make him a millionaire. He suggested that the captain build the restaurant himself, call it "Howard Johnson's," and use Johnson for his supplier. This became one of the first franchises in the country, thus qualifying Howard Johnson for the title of "Father of Franchises." Happily, the new restaurant made money from the very start.

Howard Johnson was a fanatic when it came to cleanliness. Several days a week, he made unannounced visits to the hundreds of restaurants that now bore his name. He checked the kitchens, dining rooms, and restrooms, and would explode if he found dirt, smudges, or litter anywhere.

Howard Johnson never lost his love of ice cream. Throughout his life he would eat at least one ice cream cone a day. And the freezer in his

New York penthouse never held less than ten different flavors.

"I've spent my life developing scores of flavors," he said many times, "and yet, most people still say, 'I'll take vanilla.'"

The next time you see one of those familiar restaurants or motels along the highway with the distinctive orange roof, remember the twenty-seven-year-old man who put five hundred dollars into a failing business because he wasn't afraid to take a chance.

★ William Wrigley Jr.
(Wrigley's Chewing Gum)

Thomas Adams invented chewing gum (see Chapter 8), but it was William Wrigley who persuaded the world to chew it.

William was born in Philadelphia, the oldest of nine children. His father was a soapmaker, and by the time William was ten years old, he was sent out on the streets every Saturday to sell the soap from a basket.

Having been introduced to the world of commerce, young William soon got tired of school. When he was only eleven years old, he and a friend ran away to New York City and supported themselves by doing odd jobs and selling newspapers. This lasted only a few weeks. He returned home, but not to school, where he had always gotten into trouble. His father agreed to let him work in his soap factory, but he gave his son the tough-

est job in the factory—stirring a huge vat of liquid soap. His salary was only a dollar and a half
a week.

William was very large for his age. By the
time he turned thirteen, he convinced his father
to let him go on the road as a salesman. He was
outfitted with a bright red wagon with four horses
and jingling bells.

In 1891, at the age of thirty, Wrigley moved
to Chicago with a wife, two children, and only
thirty-two dollars in his pocket. He was determined to start his own business, and an uncle,
William Scatchard, agreed to lend him five thousand dollars on the condition that he take Scatchard's son as a partner.

The two cousins began their soap business,
and Wrigley decided to give away baking powder
with each sale. When his customers seemed more
interested in the baking powder than the soap,
he switched to selling baking powder and started
giving away free chewing gum. Chewing gum was
just starting to gain popularity and his customers
were more interested in the gum than the baking
powder. Again, there was a change in direction.
In less than a year, William Wrigley's business had
switched from soap to baking powder to gum. It
never switched again.

Wrigley's first two flavors were called *Lotta
Gum* and *Vassar*. The next year he introduced
Juicy Fruit and *Spearmint*, which became the company's best-selling brand until *Doublemint* came
along in 1914.

Wrigley was a born salesman and organizer.
It wasn't long before he gained complete own-

ership of the business. At first, he contracted the Zeno Manufacturing Company to produce the chewing gum for him, but in 1911, he bought Zeno and it became the William Wrigley Jr. Company. (Wrigley never used a comma in his name.)

Advertising helped Wrigley's company go from a small local company to a national business in a matter of only a few weeks. His philosophy on advertising was "Tell 'em quick and tell 'em often."

During the depression year of 1907, the Chewing Gum King spent $250,000 on advertising. "People chew harder when they're sad," he said, and he watched the profits come in. While most businesses suffered heavy losses or went bankrupt during economic slumps, Wrigley's Chewing Gum kept Americans chomping away. "We are a five-cent business, and nobody in this company can ever afford to forget it," he said over and over again.

In later years, when he was called America's greatest salesman, Wrigley summed up his philosophy on selling with these words: "To be always pleasant, always patient, always on time, and never to argue."

When he became wealthy, Wrigley extended his interests. He bought the Chicago Cubs and built Wrigley Field for their home games. In 1919, he purchased Catalina Island, off the coast of southern California, and developed it into a pleasure resort.

When he died in 1932, *The New York Times* recorded what it called Wrigley's simple outlook on life: "I'm not much more successful than the average person. I have more money, but I've only three suits of clothes, a place to sleep, three square meals a day, and a bathtub. Maybe it's a little better bathtub."

★ 3 ★

Unusual Motives

Making money is not the only reason for starting a business or inventing a new product. Sometimes the reasons are noble, like Gail Borden's determination to protect young babies from the dangers of tainted milk (see Chapter 6). Others were spurred on by practical concerns, such as linoleum manufacturer Thomas Armstrong's need to augment his very small income (see Chapter 2).

But in some cases, very unusual motives inspired men and women to invent certain well-known products.

★ George Eastman
(Eastman Kodak Company)

George Eastman did not invent photography but
he, more than anyone else, made it possible for
anyone to own an inexpensive camera and be
able to take good pictures. In Eastman's day, taking pictures meant lugging around fifty pounds
of equipment, including a dark tent big enough
to crawl into to develop the glass plates as soon
as they had been exposed.

Eastman became interested in photography
when he started planning his first vacation from
his job as bookkeeper in a bank in his hometown
of Rochester, New York. At age twenty-three, he
was making eight hundred dollars a year, which
was considered a fairly good wage for the 1870s.

The industrious young man had worked hard
and saved his money, and now he wanted to
spend some of his savings to see the world. For
months he talked of nothing else but a vacation
to Santo Domingo. A friend at the bank suggested that George buy some photographic
equipment so he could take pictures of the Central American jungles.

Eastman thought that was a good idea. His
mother could then share the trip through the
photographs he brought back. Cameras were as
big as some microwave ovens, and they had to be
placed on tripods that were strong and heavy. Instead of film, glass plates were used. The plates
were coated with silver nitrate, exposed in the
camera while they were still wet, and developed

on the spot before they dried. This required many bottles of chemicals, glass tanks, a heavy plate holder, and a jug of water—not to mention a lightproof tent for developing the glass images.

Friends would tease Eastman when he set out on expeditions to test the equipment and his developing techniques. After all the trouble and expense he had gone through, however, he gave up his plans for a Santo Domingo vacation. He did get to visit the Great Lakes, though, and took excellent photographs to show his mother and friends at work.

It wasn't long before Eastman became more interested in photography than banking. His hobby became a passion, though he believed there had to be a more efficient method of taking pictures.

He read in British magazines that photographers were experimenting with gelatin emulsions that would remain sensitive when dry and would not have to be exposed and developed immediately. Although he had never studied chemistry, Eastman began to experiment in his mother's kitchen. He would work in the bank during the day and mix emulsions all night. There were some nights that he worked straight through until dawn. His mother began leaving a blanket and pillow by the stove, but he rarely used them. Finally, he developed a dry plate that satisfied him.

At first, he intended to make dry plates just for his own use. Then he saw the potential for a profitable business. He built a machine that could turn out large numbers of his new dry plates and rented space in a building in the middle of town.

Then came the momentous decision. He would leave his job at the bank and go into the dry-plate business. Within a year, he was turning out four thousand plates a month.

George Eastman's big break came when he invented a strip of paper that would hold the sensitized gelatin emulsion. Eastman called his new product *film*—the first in photographic history.

In 1888, after three years of work, Eastman introduced a small, lightweight box camera that could be held in the hands rather than set on a tripod. It was so simple to use that *anyone* could take pictures, even children. The twenty-five-dollar camera came with enough film for one hundred pictures, and after the photographs were taken, the camera would be mailed back to the Eastman company. For ten dollars, the film was developed, prints made, and the camera returned with film for one hundred more pictures. In 1889 Eastman began marketing transparent film in rolls.

George Eastman had provided Americans with a camera and film that were affordable and easy to use. All that was lacking was a good brand name for the product. He wanted a name that was unique and catchy, something short and snappy. He sat down with a piece of paper and pencil and started to doodle. He found himself writing the letter *k* over and over again. It had always been his favorite letter of the alphabet.

How about a word that began and ended with *k*? After several attempts at different combinations, he came up with the word *Kodak*.

Taking "snapshots" became a new pastime.

In 1890, the first folding Kodak camera was introduced. In 1900, the first Brownie camera came out. It cost only one dollar, and a roll of film was only fifteen cents. Now anyone could afford to take pictures. And it was all made possible because one man decided he didn't want to lug around fifty pounds of equipment on his back.

Today, George Eastman is remembered almost as much for his charitable contributions as for his contributions to the field of photography.

The Massachusetts Institute of Technology, for instance, received an anonymous gift of twenty million dollars from George Eastman because he admired the quality of their graduates, many of whom had come to work for Eastman Kodak. A thirty-million-dollar gift was given to Hampton and Tuskegee Institutes.

In his hometown of Rochester, New York, Eastman provided the funds for a dental clinic for children and contributed heavily to the University of Rochester's medical school and hospital. Because music was absent from his early years, Eastman provided guidance and financial support for the Eastman School of Music, the Eastman Theatre, and the Rochester Symphony Orchestra.

For George Eastman, great wealth brought him a greater opportunity to serve mankind.

★ Edwin Land
(Polaroid Land Camera)

If you have ever worn a pair of polarized sunglasses, you know that they can eliminate glare. Take a photograph of a plate-glass window and all you get is the reflection in the glass; put a polarized filter on the camera lens, and the picture of the window will show what is on the inside without any glare.

Edwin Land was only eighteen years old and a student at Harvard in 1928 when he began experimenting with light waves. He soon discovered a method of polarizing light. Convinced that the auto industry would use his polarized sheets for sun visors and headlights, he quit school to continue his experiments. It took nine years to perfect his product, but car makers were no longer interested when they learned that the treated polyvinyl sheets could not tolerate heat.

The company he founded in 1937 began making sunglasses instead. When the United States entered World War II, there was a demand for goggles, glasses, and filters. The Polaroid Company did well until the war ended and business dropped off once again. In 1947, the firm lost two million dollars, and Land desperately needed a new product to sell. Then he remembered an incident that had taken place a few years before.

Edwin Land had taken some time off from work to enjoy a brief vacation in Santa Fe, New Mexico. Like all tourists, he had taken his camera with him. When he snapped a picture of his three-year-old daughter, she asked how long it would take before she could see it. That innocent question started the inventor thinking: Would it be possible to develop and print photographs *inside* the camera?

Land became obsessed with the idea. It took only a few hours to come up with the basic principles for the camera, the film, and the chemistry needed to make it all possible. It took four years, however, to translate those ideas into practical reality.

In 1947, Edwin Land startled the photographic world when he introduced the *Land Polaroid Model 95*, a four-pound camera that produced sepia-toned pictures in sixty seconds. The camera was priced to sell for $89.75.

Instant photography proved to be an instant success. But there would be many improvements on both the camera and the film in the following years: fifteen-second pictures and automatic exposure in 1963, color film and film cartridges in 1963, the low-priced *Swinger* in 1965, and the popular *Square Shooter* in 1971.

Although Edwin Land never returned to college to finish his education, he holds more than a dozen honorary degrees. With 524 U.S. patents in his name, he was inducted into the patent office's National Inventors Hall of Fame in 1977.

★ Dorothy Gerber
(Gerber Baby Food)

Up until the late 1920s, when babies graduated
from liquid diets to solid food their mothers had
to strain the food by hand. This was a time-
consuming process and had to be done every day.

Mrs. Dan Gerber knew the process very well.
She had performed the daily ritual for her oldest
daughter, Scotti, until she was able to chew her
own food. Then a second child, Sally, was born
and Mrs. Gerber had to start all over again.

One summer evening in 1927, Dan Gerber
walked into the kitchen and sat at the table
watching his three-year-old feed herself while his
wife was at the counter straining peas for the
baby. Dorothy turned to her husband and asked
him why his father's cannery couldn't do the job
for her. After all, the Freemont Canning Company in Michigan had been processing food for
many years.

To press her point, Dorothy Gerber dumped
a whole container of peas into a strainer and
bowl, placed them in her husband's lap, and asked
him to see how he'd like to do that three times a
day, seven days a week.

The next day, Dan was in his father's office
to ask if the baby's vegetables could be strained
at the plant. Frank Gerber, who was not only a
doting grandfather but an astute businessman,
saw the possibility of pleasing not only his
daughter-in-law but young mothers everywhere.

Many months were spent developing production techniques and recipes so the new product could be produced at a reasonable cost. Doctors, nutritionists, and home economists were consulted. Finally, in the fall of 1928, *Gerber Strained Baby Foods* appeared on the market. The first five products were carrots, peas, prunes, spinach, and vegetable soup. Although weary mothers across the land welcomed the news, the Gerbers knew that it would take a concentrated advertising campaign to convince money-conscious shoppers that the convenience was worth the cost.

Dan Gerber wanted a picture of a healthy, happy baby to illustrate his national ads. Leading artists were invited to submit paintings for consideration. Just before the deadline, an artist named Dorothy Hope submitted a small unfinished charcoal sketch of her neighbor's child. "If this baby is the right age and size," she told the Gerbers, "I'll go ahead with the painting."

The fresh, appealing sketch immediately won the hearts of all those who saw it, and the Gerber Baby was born. It was also agreed that the humble drawing should remain in its unfinished state. The Gerber Baby has appeared on every Gerber label and in every Gerber ad since it was first adopted as the company's official trademark in 1931.

Today, Gerber offers approximately 150 different products in the United States. Gerber baby foods are also available in 160 countries, with labels printed in ten languages. Gerber's trademark is truly "the best-known baby in the world."

★ Dr. Benjamin Franklin Goodrich
(B. F. Goodrich Tires)

By the end of the nineteenth century, Akron, Ohio, had become the rubber capital of the world. Dr. Goodrich was the first rubber manufacturer to set up business there.

How did a Civil War surgeon get into the rubber business? Goodrich saw a friend's house completely destroyed by fire because the leather hoses had burst. Leather tended to dry out and become brittle in a short time. Goodrich was convinced that rubber would make a better fire hose.

Although it had been over thirty years since Charles Goodyear had accidentally discovered the process for treating rubber (see Chapter 8), there were few uses for the substance and most of the rubber items being made were of poor quality. In addition to fire and garden hoses, Goodrich could see the need for rubber hoses to transport oil and for numerous applications in surgical and medical equipment.

Dr. Goodrich came closer to realizing his dreams when he and a business partner started making loans to a small rubber company in New York State. The Hudson River Rubber Company was having financial troubles. By 1869, Goodrich and his partner had become full owners.

The location and condition of the plant would not permit product development, so Goodrich decided to start a new firm in the Midwest, where production costs would be lower. He chose Akron, Ohio, a town of ten thousand, with two canals, two railroads, a coal mine, and a large number of skilled immigrants from Central Europe.

By May of the following year, a newly erected and equipped factory building was turning out hoses, gaskets, bottle stoppers, jar rings, and wringers for washing machines. Before the end of the first year, Dr. Goodrich had developed the world's first cotton-covered rubber fire hose, which became the forerunner of the pneumatic tire.

Those tires appeared on the first automobile manufactured for commercial sale, built by Alexander Winton in 1896. They were made, of course, by the B. F. Goodrich Company.

Quality and new inventions became the hallmarks of Dr. Goodrich's company as he raised the standards of the entire rubber industry.

★ King Camp Gillette
(Gillette Razors)

King Gillette was on his own from the time he was seventeen, when the Chicago fire wiped out his father's business. At twenty-one, he was earning his living as a traveling salesman and dreaming of inventing something—though he didn't know what.

The young man became friends with William Painter, who had invented the product Gillette was selling. The cork-lined tin bottle cap, known as the Crown Cork, was used on almost all beer and soft drink bottles sold in America. Painter encouraged young Gillette to come up with a similar type of product—something people used once, then threw away. Gillette became obsessed with the challenge.

Every waking minute, he looked for the inspiration that would make him wealthy. He even went through the alphabet and listed every need imaginable, but he couldn't think of anything that had to be thrown away after just one use.

One morning as he began to shave, he discovered that his razor was not only dull, but beyond the point of sharpening on the leather strop. He would have to take it to a barber or cutlery shop to have it honed.

As he stood before the mirror with the razor in his hand, he felt a light go on in his head. "If a thin piece of steel with two sharp edges were placed between two clamping plates attached to a handle, a man could get a close shave and throw away the blade when it got dull." In that flash of inspiration, the disposable razor blade was invented.

That very day Gillette wrote to his wife, who was visiting friends in Ohio. "I have it," he penned. "Our fortune is made!" But fame and wealth were not to come that easily.

It took eleven years of hard work and endless experiments before he could make a single dollar on his invention. The problem was to find a way of manufacturing steel into ribbons thin enough and of sufficient quality to guarantee a clean shave at an affordable price.

In 1900, William E. Nickerson entered the

picture. A graduate of the Massachusetts Institute of Technology, Nickerson succeeded in developing a process for hardening and sharpening sheet steel.

Gillette persuaded some friends to invest five thousand dollars in his new company, and manufacture of the razors began. In 1903, the *Gillette Safety Razor* was introduced. Only 51 razors and 168 blades were sold that first year, but the following year, sales leaped to 91,000 razors and 123,000 blades. There seemed to be no end in sight.

When the United States entered World War I, Gillette's output went almost exclusively to the armed forces. Men who had still been using straight razors were introduced to the Gillette safety razor, and most never went back to the old way of shaving.

The company's trademark was King Gillette's face and signature. The familiar face on the front of every pack of blades was reproduced more than one hundred billion times, probably making it one of the most widely reproduced portraits in history.

★ George Safford Parker
(Parker Pens)

Communication was both vocation and avocation for George Parker. The Wisconsin native taught telegraphy in the town of Janesville. As a hobby, he studied people's basic need to express themselves. When the twenty-five-year-old looked for a way to make more money, it wasn't surprising that he decided to sell fountain pens, a basic instrument of communication.

Parker made a deal with a manufacturer in Ohio, and had no trouble selling a shipment of pens to his students. But when the pens began to leak and Parker spent a lot of time trying to repair them, he vowed to create a leak-proof fountain pen.

After a careful study of fountain pens and their construction, as well as the principles of capillary action, Parker designed a new feed bar, the mechanism that supplies ink from the rubber reservoir to the point. Two years after he introduced his instrument, the Parker Pen Company was formed. At the time, only five percent of the literate population of the United States owned fountain pens. George Parker set out to change that.

Parker traveled extensively around the country and eventually introduced his superior product to Europe, Asia, and Australia. "Remember," he told his associates, "our pens will write in any language."

When America entered World War I, a real boom in letter writing took place. By 1918, when the war ended, the company had chalked up its first million dollar sales year. It eventually became one of the world's leading manufacturers of pens.

The man who said, "I can make a better pen," would have been pleased to learn that some of history's most important documents were signed with his creation. Presidents Franklin D. Roosevelt and Harry S. Truman, and Generals Dwight D. Eisenhower and Douglas MacArthur, all used Parker pens. Carl Sandburg recorded history, George Bernard Shaw created *Pygmalion*, and Sir Arthur Conan Doyle wrote some of his Sherlock Holmes stories with Parker pens.

After decades of using throw-away ballpoint pens, today people are beginning to use fountain pens again. But there is one major difference. They used to cost anywhere from one dollar to ten dollars. Today, the price tag can be as high as eighty dollars to one hundred dollars.

★ Dr. William M. Scholl
(Dr. Scholl's Foot Care Products)

William Scholl was born in 1882 and grew up on his parents' dairy farm near LaPort, Indiana, one of thirteen children. Milking cows was not one of his favorite chores; his mind was focused on more creative pursuits.

When he was only fifteen, Scholl designed and sewed a complete set of harnesses for his father's horses. He made his own waxed thread and cut all the straps from a full side of leather. The remarkable task required over one hundred thousand stitches!

His father was so impressed with his son's accomplishment that the young man was made the family's cobbler. He designed and stitched

shoes for his parents and his twelve brothers and
sisters.

At sixteen, Billy Scholl was apprenticed to
the local shoemaker, but he soon became restless.
Within a year, he decided to leave LaPort and
look for opportunities elsewhere. He moved to
Chicago and got a job in a shoe store. He proved
that he had learned his trade well by making and
fitting shoes to misshapen feet. He also turned
out to be an exceptionally fine salesman.

For the first time, Scholl realized how many
people in America were suffering from bunions,
corns, and fallen arches. Feet were being ne-
glected, he concluded, and neither doctors nor
shoemakers were doing anything about it. His
concern led him to quit his job at the shoe store
and enroll at the Illinois Medical College, taking
a night job to pay the bills. In addition to the
regular curriculum, he read everything he could
find on the subject of feet.

By the time he received his M.D. degree in
1904, the twenty-two-year-old Dr. Scholl had invented and patented his first arch support. When
he slipped his first handmade arch support into
a customer's shoe, the joyful man stomped
around the store and exclaimed, "That's a real
foot easer, isn't it?" With that spontaneous reac-
tion, the world's first arch support got its name.

From the very beginning, *Foot-Eazers* have
been one of Dr. Scholl's best-selling items. The
self-appointed foot doctor to the world continued
to develop and add more products to the company's line. Today, there are over a thousand, and

not one was ever discontinued during Scholl's lifetime.

Dr. Scholl was considered an eccentric by many. When he made sales calls, he would often pull out a skeleton of a human foot from a specially built pocket in his coat for dramatic effect.

William Scholl died a bachelor in 1968 at the age of eighty-six, having had only one corn in his entire life. *Time* magazine, in its obituary, called him "the first bunion millionaire."

★ Alexander Graham Bell
   (Bell Telephone Co.)

Alexander Bell (the name Graham was added later) was born in Edinburgh, Scotland, in 1847, into a family of well-known elocutionists—those who teach proper speech. His father had even developed a system for teaching speech to deaf people.

Young Alexander and his two brothers were educated to follow in the family tradition. When both brothers died at an early age from tuberculosis, their father decided to move his family to North America to protect the health of his only surviving son.

In his new surroundings in Ontario, Canada, Alexander showed a gift for teaching the deaf to speak. By the age of twenty-five, he had opened his own school in Boston, Massachusetts, to train teachers to work with the deaf. A year later, he became a professor at the University of Boston.

It was only natural that Alexander Bell should become interested in finding a way to transmit the human voice over long distances. Several others had done research along these lines, especially since the invention of the telegraph, but transmitting sounds that could be *understood* had yet to be achieved.

After several failed attempts, Bell realized that he was a specialist in acoustics, not electrical engineering. Then one day, in the shop where he bought his electrical equipment, he met a young and brilliant electrical engineer named Thomas Watson. Intuitively, Bell knew that this was the man who could help him turn his ideas into reality. Watson accepted Bell's challenge and the two began the long experiments that would eventually lead to the first practical telephone.

On March 10, 1876, Alexander Bell sent his assistant the first telephone message ever transmitted over a wire: "Mr. Watson, come here. I want you." Those seven historic words have been etched for all time in the annals of history. What has been forgotten was the reason for those words—the inventor had just spilled a beaker of acid down the front of his trousers.

Another inventor, named Elisha Gray, was also developing a device for transmitting the voice. In fact, the two were so similar that a battle for patent rights began as soon as Bell's telephone was introduced to the public. After many court hearings, Bell's patents were upheld by the Supreme Court in 1893. By that time, the telephone had already become a valuable means of communication in many countries.

Bell's name is still used to identify most local telephone companies. But the creator, who used his royalties to establish what is now known as the Alexander Graham Bell Association for the Deaf, once said that he would rather be remembered as a teacher of the deaf than as the inventor of the telephone.

★ Joseph Pulitzer
(Pulitzer Prizes)

Joseph Pulitzer was known for sensationalism and muckraking in newspaper reporting. Along with his arch rival, William Randolph Hearst, Pulitzer made the phrase "yellow journalism" part of the American vocabulary during his coverage of the Spanish-American War.

At the age of seventeen, Hungarian-born Joseph Pulitzer emigrated to the United States. The year was 1864 and America was engaged in the Civil War. The young adventurer was soon fighting with the First New York Cavalry.

In 1867, Pulitzer became an American citizen and landed a job on a German newspaper in St. Louis, Missouri. It wasn't long before he became managing editor and part owner of the paper.

After time out to study for and receive a law degree, Joseph Pulitzer returned to journalism. He bought two failing St. Louis newspapers and combined them to form the *Post-Dispatch*. Five years later, he also became the owner of the New York *World*.

Under Pulitzer's management, the *World* became well known for its sensational style of reporting, including exposés, crusades against corruption, and a strong editorial position in favor of labor. The crusading publisher gave new meaning to the word "muckraking." It may have been because of this well-deserved reputation that Pulitzer decided to help others pursue careers in investigative journalism.

In his will, Joseph Pulitzer left two million dollars to Columbia University for the purpose of founding a graduate school of journalism. He specified that five hundred thousand dollars of that sum should be used to establish and maintain annual prizes for distinguished work in writing and journalism. The awards were to be bestowed by Columbia's trustees and administered by the Graduate School of Journalism.

Long after the yellow pages of his newspapers have faded into oblivion, the name Joseph Pulitzer lives on in the prizes his wealth made possible.

★ 4 ★

Struggles

Consider the kite. It doesn't rise *with* the wind, but *against* it. Eliminate the tension by letting go of the string and the kite will plunge to the ground. The same is true in human lives. Very little that is worthwhile is accomplished without some effort.

The caterpillar is another good example. It struggles to get out of its cocoon, but once it is free, the new butterfly flaps its multicolored wings and takes off. If someone were to feel sorry for the struggling butterfly and cut the cocoon open, it would flit around for a moment and then die. Struggle is part of life.

Difficulties, hardships, and trials can strengthen the human spirit and create the self-reliance that is needed to face more struggles down the road.

Most of the entrepreneurs who left their "brand" on America encountered some failures before they found success. The fourteen individuals whose stories are told in this chapter faced more than their share of struggles. But like the butterfly and the kite, they were finally able to "take off" and realize their dreams.

★ Carl A. Swanson
(Swanson's Frozen Dinners)

In 1896, a seventeen-year-old immigrant arrived in this country without a penny in his pocket. As he stepped off the boat, he wore a sign around his neck which read: "Carl Swanson, Swedish. Send me to Omaha. I speak no English."

The friendly young immigrant worked hard, taking any job he could find. Within three years, he had not only learned to speak English but had saved enough money to buy a share in a wholesale food company. It wasn't long before he had bought out his partner and owned the company outright. In the late 1920s, he switched to food processing.

When television burst upon the American scene in the late 1940s, life-styles suddenly changed. Instead of eating at the dining room table, many families sat in front of the television set in the living room and ate off trays. Mothers didn't want to be stuck in the kitchen preparing meals, so Swanson's food processing company came to the rescue.

Carl Swanson died in 1949, but he passed control of his business on to his sons Gilbert and Clarke. In 1953 they introduced *Swanson's TV Dinners*. This was the first time the frozen food industry provided fully cooked dinners that just needed to be heated in the oven.

Four decades after Carl Swanson had landed on these shores, the industry he had started was doing thirty-three million dollars' worth of business every year. Swanson's sons continued the legacy, making their name a household word. For this family especially, America really was the land of opportunity.

★ Alfred Carl Fuller
(Fuller Brushes)

Although he grew up in Nova Scotia, Canada, Alfred Fuller claimed that his ancestors had come over on the Mayflower. It was his great-great-great-grandfather who had accepted Nova Scotia's grant of free land in 1761, fifteen years before the birth of the United States.

Alfred, born in 1885, was the eleventh of twelve children. He got his formal education in a one-room schoolhouse, his vocational training on the family farm, and his religious instruction from his Methodist mother. School was not one of his favorite activities, though, and he dropped out before the seventh grade.

Following the lead of his siblings who had already crossed the border and settled near Boston, Alfred Fuller came to the United States with little money and few possessions. He managed to get fired from three consecutive jobs, which would have discouraged most people, but Alfred Fuller was ready for something new. He landed a sales job with the Somerville Brush and Mop Company. One of his brothers, who had started the business, was moving west and recommended Alfred to the new owner.

It wasn't long before Fuller made two discoveries. First, he found out that he was a natural salesman. In fact, he could sell brushes that did not even exist. If a housewife asked for a brush to perform a particular household task, he would select any brush from his sample case that he thought would do the job, and the customer would buy it.

The second discovery was that wire-twisted brushes looked easy to make. If he bought a wire-twisting machine, some spools of galvanized wire, and a supply of horsehair and hog bristles, he knew he could make his own brushes and pocket all the profit.

After he had saved up some money, the budding entrepreneur quit his job, spent eighty dollars on supplies and equipment, and on New Year's Day, 1906, set up shop in his sister's basement.

Fuller decided to limit himself to the seven basic types of brushes that were most in demand. He went from door to door taking orders during the day and making the brushes at night. This eliminated the need for keeping an inventory on hand. Each brush took only fifteen minutes to make with a few cents' worth of material. He sold them for fifty cents each.

By the time the Fuller Brush Company was formed in 1910, there were twenty-five salesmen and six brush makers. The following year, the small-scale brush manufacturer became a nationwide operation when hundreds of people answered newspaper ads to be agents for the company. Like an invading army, there were soon thousands of well-groomed salesmen with sample cases in hand, ringing doorbells in big cities and small towns all across the nation.

"The Fuller Brush Man," as he was called, would offer the housewife a gift and wait to be invited in. The free "handy brush" was the enticement that opened the door to a carefully prepared sales talk and, more often than not, an order for several brushes. Detergents, vacuum cleaners, and other laborsaving devices had not yet been invented, so specially designed brushes were a must to reach all the dust-catching nooks and crannies of late–nineteenth-century homes.

The Fuller Brush Company received more free publicity than any other business of its day. The Fuller Brush Man was even a favorite subject of comedians. Radio comic Fred Allen once said, "Edison gave us the electric light, Marconi gave us the wireless, and Fuller gave us the brush." The persistent Fuller Brush Man also turned up in many magazine cartoons.

The ultimate tribute came in the late 1940s when the popular comedian Red Skelton starred in a movie called *The Fuller Brush Man*. That kind of publicity was worth millions to the company that began with an eighty-dollar investment by a young man who, if he had finished school, might have been voted "Least Likely to Succeed."

★ Amanda Smith
   (Mrs. Smith's Pies)

It's easy these days to be a good cook. All you have to do is buy a frozen pie that is ready for the oven and heat it for the prescribed amount of time; then you can truthfully say that you "baked" the pie.

Amanda Smith never dreamed that her pies would be known across the land when she began baking commercially in 1919 in the little town of Pottstown, Pennsylvania. She was a widow looking for a way to support herself and her family.

Smith's seventeen-year-old son, Robert, operated a lunch counter in the local YMCA and he suggested that his mother supply the pies, which were an instant hit. Her baking provided a modest income, but finances got tight when Robert left the lunch counter to go to college.

Robert, however, dropped out of school and devoted all of his time to selling his mother's pies to local grocery stores and restaurants. When business picked up, the baking operation moved from the family kitchen to a small store in town.

Amanda Smith went into semi-retirement in 1925, the same year that the bakery was incorporated. Although she is long gone, the pies that bear

her name can be found in supermarket freezers
all over the country.

★ David Dunbar Buick
(Buick Automobiles)

It is ironic that David Buick is remembered for
his biggest failure—making automobiles. No one
remembers that Buick invented a process for fus-
ing porcelain onto cast iron to make sinks and
other bathroom fixtures. A bathtub by Buick became a prized possession in many homes in the
1880s. When he switched to making automobiles,
he was soon "washed up."

David Buick was born in Scotland in 1854
and was brought to the United States when he
was only two. His parents settled in Detroit, and
when his father died three years later, the family
was plunged into poverty. David had to drop out
of school at eleven and went to work as a farm
hand.

With the mechanical skills he picked up on
the farm, young David apprenticed himself at the
age of fifteen to a company that made brass and
iron castings and fire hydrants. In his spare time,
he experimented with the porcelain bonding
process.

When he made the breakthrough and patented his discovery, he and another apprentice
quit their jobs and formed the Buick and Sherwood Company. At age twenty-eight, David Buick
felt he was a success as his company turned out

enameled bathtubs and, eventually, a full line of
plumbing fixtures.

Within ten years, he was a prosperous businessman with prospects of making millions. Then
a strange thing happened. Buick suddenly lost interest in bathtubs and fell in love with the internal combustion engine. He sold his half of Buick
and Sherwood to the Standard Sanitary Manufacturing Company (still a well-known name in
bathroom fixtures) and formed a company to
make engines.

With the hundred thousand dollars he had
gotten from the sale, Buick hired a French-born
engineer named Eugene Richard to design and
build an automobile. Richard invented a valve-
in-head engine, which produced greater power
and a faster burn. The patent was taken out in
Richard's name, and the engine was installed in a
chassis designed by David Buick and called the
Buick Model F.

In 1903, the Buick Motor Company was organized, but the design and construction of the
first car had taken all of Buick's capital and he
was deeply in debt. A carriage maker from Flint,
Michigan, by the name of William Crapo Durant
stepped in and bought the company.

Durant was a business genius. With his know-
how, Buick sales began to soar, and by 1908, the
Buick plant was the biggest automobile factory in
the world. That year, Durant used the success of
Buick to buy Cadillac, Oldsmobile, and a number
of smaller companies and formed General Motors.

One of the early presidents of the Buick

Motor Company was a man who later went on to start his own automobile company—Walter Chrysler.

As for David Buick, he became involved in several other ill-fated business ventures and sank into debt. Before his death in 1929, he worked as a clerk at a Detroit vocational school. He was poorly paid and, by then, virtually forgotten.

Though Buick never realized his dreams, his name eventually became synonymous with quality in American automobiles and was immortalized in the famous slogan: "Wouldn't you really rather drive a Buick?"

★ Milton S. Hershey
(Hershey's Chocolate)

Like father, like son. That's what they all said about young Milton Hershey, who was born in 1857. But it was not meant to be a compliment. Milton's father, Henry, was very different from the other Mennonite farmers who lived in the region known as Pennsylvania Dutch country. They believed in hard work, religious devotion, and a simple life-style. Henry, however, dabbled in candymaking and dreamed of being an artist. His ever-changing interests kept his wife and son in poverty and ended Milton's formal education at the fourth grade.

Milton was well into his thirties before he experienced anything resembling success. Following in his father's footsteps, he learned the art of candymaking, but his apprenticeship in a local confectioner's store was a disaster. At nineteen, he set up shop in Philadelphia during the centennial celebration of the Declaration of Independence in 1876. He made candy at night and sold it during the day, but the long hours were too much for him and his health soon suffered.

The lure of silver brought father and son to Colorado, but instead of striking it rich, Milton ended up as a candymaker's helper in Denver until he could earn enough money to move on. And move on they did, to Chicago and New Orleans, where their attempts to make and sell candy led once again to failure.

Instead of being discouraged, Henry Hershey was convinced that he had been too timid in his business ventures. "If you want to make money," he told his son, "you must do things in a large way." So off they went to New York City.

Henry Hershey had just developed a cough drop formula that he just knew would be their ticket to success. The Mennonite farmer and his son made a valiant attempt to conquer the big city, but after several years, their world came crashing down in the biggest defeat of all.

Henry Hershey stayed in New York to see if he could sell some of his paintings. Milton returned home without a penny in his pocket. He had to borrow money from an aunt so he could start again, making candy at night and selling it by day from a basket on his arm.

There was a difference this time, though. The milk caramels he made had a unique flavor because of a secret he had learned while in Denver—the use of fresh milk improved the taste. Candy lovers agreed and the demand for his fresh milk caramels gave Milton Hershey his first taste of success. Then, a lucky coincidence boosted his sales even more. A candy importer from England sampled Hershey's caramels and gave him a sizable order.

Within a few years, a large caramel factory was built in Lancaster, Pennsylvania, and the successful candymaker thought the time was right to think of marriage. In 1898, at the age of forty-one, Milton Hershey surprised his family and friends by marrying Catherine Sweeney of Jamestown, New York. He had met the young girl in a candy shop where she worked.

Two years later, Hershey made what appeared to be a reckless move. He sold his successful Lancaster Caramel Company for one million dollars. He wasn't tired of candymaking and he didn't intend to sit back and enjoy retirement. Instead, he turned his attention to milk chocolate.

The manufacture of milk chocolate was a complicated process, but Hershey felt there was a demand for the confection that was not being met. At the time, chocolate candy was expensive and sold only in large blocks. Hershey's idea was to mass-produce the milk chocolate, wrap it in pocket-sized bars that could sell for a nickel, and make it available in every food store, restaurant, drugstore, ice cream parlor, and soda fountain in the United States.

To accomplish his dream, in 1905 Hershey built a chocolate factory in the middle of a field

near his birthplace of Derry Church. The clean
and efficient dairy farms nearby would guarantee
a steady supply of fresh milk, and the industrious
Pennsylvania Dutch people would make an ideal
work force.

Surrounding the chocolate factory, Milton
Hershey envisioned a beautiful town in which his
workers could live and raise their families. He
began by offering financial assistance to any employee who wanted to build a new home. Eventually, Hershey built a community center, a sports
stadium, schools, and a medical center in the rapidly growing town, whose name was changed to
Hershey in 1906.

Meanwhile, the five-cent Hershey Bars became an instant success. In only a few short years,
the company was selling five million dollars'
worth of chocolate a year—all without the benefit
of advertising. Hershey believed that the best kind
of advertising was a quality product. He must
have been right, because the company's first
newspaper ads did not appear until 1970, a full
sixty-five years after the business began.

After a long series of failures, Milton Hershey finally had everything he had hoped for, with
one exception. He and his wife remained child-
less. He remedied that by establishing a school
for orphaned children. Later, he left his prosperous business to the school, which still owns the
giant Hershey Foods Corporation today.

As a Mennonite, Hershey had been taught
that money was not to be used for personal grat-
ification. By living out that belief, Milton Hershey
became one of an elite group of successful busi-

nessmen who gave away most of their millions to
enrich the lives of others.

★ Frank Winfield Woolworth
   (F. W. Woolworth Co.)

As a young boy growing up on his father's farm
in the late 1850's in Rodman, New York, and later
in Grand Bend, Frank Woolworth would often
play store with his younger brother after the farm
chores were done. They would set up a display of
items on the dining table (anything they could
find in the house) and "sell" their merchandise
to imaginary customers.

   Even at that young age, Frank knew he
wanted to be a storekeeper. But his father was a
farmer and Frank was expected to follow the
family tradition. Although he was a good student
in the one-room schoolhouse he attended, he left
school at sixteen to work full-time with his father.
He disliked the rough, heavy farm work and the
bitter-cold winters of upstate New York. Whenever he could, he took some courses at a local
business school.

   At the age of twenty-one, Woolworth landed
a job with a leading dry-goods store in nearby
Watertown, New York. For the first three months
he received no salary as he swept floors, delivered
packages, and arranged window displays. When
he finally went on the payroll, Frank Woolworth
was paid $3.50 for a six-day, eighty-four-hour
week. And so he labored for the next six years.

Woolworth thought he was on the road to success when he went to work for another dry-goods store at the grand salary of ten dollars a week, but his struggles were not over. His new employer told him he was a poor salesman and cut his salary to eight dollars a month. Woolworth's response was to work even harder, but the new pace was too much for him. He suffered a complete breakdown and lost his job as well as half a year of his life trying to regain his strength.

After his recovery and marriage to a young Canadian girl who worked as a seamstress in Watertown, Woolworth's life seemed to take a turn for the better. His first employer had taken a new partner and asked Woolworth to come back to the store. He did, and his attractive window displays were soon bringing in new customers.

These were difficult years following the Civil War. Merchants were looking for innovative ways to get rid of the unsold merchandise that lined their shelves. One sales ploy that became popular was the "five-cent counter," which featured a variety of items marked down to a nickel. The fad soon passed because so many of these items were shoddy and there wasn't much variety.

Woolworth changed that when he was asked to set up a five-cent counter at the store where he worked. Instead of dumping all the store's unwanted merchandise on a table, he persuaded his bosses to order one hundred dollars' worth of safety pins, combs, thimbles, buttonhooks, pencils, baby bibs, soap, and bright red napkins. He covered a long table with a calico cloth and arranged the notions with great care. He then added some of the surplus stock that had been gathering dust in the store. Over the display, he hung a handmade sign that read "Any Article on This Counter Five Cents."

The sale had been planned for the opening day of the Jefferson County Fair. When the doors opened, the five-cent counter was swept clean in a matter of hours. As Frank Woolworth watched eager shoppers pick up the inexpensive items, he resolved that he would open his own store and sell only five-cent items.

When he told his employers about his dream, they decided to help the likable young man who had done so much for them. They agreed to loan him three hundred dollars' worth of merchandise, provided he open his store in another town. They didn't want him as a competitor.

Woolworth moved to Utica, New York, and opened his "Great Five Cent Store" in 1879. The store got off to a good start and prospered for several weeks, but it was located on a little-traveled side street and it eventually failed.

Taking the advice of a friend, he moved to Lancaster, Pennsylvania, home of the thrifty Pennsylvania Dutch, who always appreciated a good bargain. When his train pulled into town early one evening, he knew he had come to the right place. There were lots of shoppers strolling the streets.

Early the next morning, Woolworth found a vacant store and quickly rented it for thirty dollars a month. It wasn't long before he was ready to open with over four hundred dollars' worth of inexpensive merchandise, all to be sold for just a nickel.

Without benefit of advertising, Woolworth opened the door for the first day of business and waited for the shoppers, who did not show up. He later said that it was the worst morning of his entire life.

What he didn't know was that the circus was coming to town that morning and everyone in town was watching the traditional circus parade. However, when the parade was over, hundreds of people found their way to Woolworth's Five Cent Store and in no time bought up one-third of his stock. In a matter of hours, 2,553 nickel purchases had been made for a grand total of $127.65. To Frank Woolworth, it seemed like a fortune.

A year later, the sign over the store was changed to "5 and 10 ¢ Store" and eventually to "Woolworth's 5 and 10 ¢ Store."

Frank Woolworth's life had been one struggle after another, but when he died in 1919, five days short of his sixty-seventh birthday, the five-cent merchant had amassed a personal fortune estimated at 65 million dollars. There were over one thousand stores around the country bearing the Woolworth name, including the Woolworth Building in Manhattan, then the tallest building in the world, for which he had paid $13.5 million in cash!

At his death, the New York *Sun* summarized his life with these words: "He won a fortune, not in showing how little could be sold for much, but how much could be sold for little."

★ Elisha Otis
(Otis Elevators)

With the exception of the automobile, it has been estimated that people travel more miles in elevators every day in this country than in all the trains, buses, and planes combined. If the safety elevator had not been invented, buildings might not be taller than five or six floors. Vertical transportation has had a dramatic effect on architecture and the way people live and work.

The next time you step off an elevator, look down at the metal track in the floor where the door slides shut and you will probably see the name *Otis*. When he introduced his invention in 1852, it looked like Elisha Otis was finally on his way up. It was about time. During the first forty years of his life, the mechanic had failed in four ill-fated business ventures—a gristmill, a carriage shop, a sawmill, and a machine shop.

In 1851, Otis got a job as a master mechanic in a New Jersey factory that made beds. The factory occupied two floors, and the owner asked Otis if he could design and build a mechanical hoist to move material and finished beds from one level to the other.

Hand-powered elevators had been in existence for several centuries, but they were very unreliable. These crude devices were raised and lowered by ropes that often broke, sending freight and any unlucky person who happened to be aboard crashing to the ground.

Elisha Otis's idea was to attach two metal devices on each side of the rising platform that would pop out and brake the elevator if the rope should break. As simple as the braking device was, it worked.

The safety elevator was truly revolutionary, but the inventor evidently did not see its potential. He installed his creation in the factory, his boss was happy, and that seemed to be the end of it.

Then, one day, a furniture manufacturer in New York City wrote to order two of Otis's safety elevators. He had just experienced a serious elevator accident in his plant. For the first time, Otis realized that his invention might have a market.

Two unrelated events occurred in the next two years that helped the Otis Elevator Company get off the ground. First, the bedstead company went out of business. This allowed Otis to build his elevators in the same factory where the first one had been put together. Then, when no more orders were forthcoming, the New York World's Fair of 1854 was about to open. This gave Otis the ideal setting to demonstrate his revolutionary invention.

With the flair of a showman, Otis set up his safety elevator in the middle of the magnificent Crystal Palace, which had been built for the exposition. Day after day, as astonished fairgoers watched, Otis stood on the big platform of the lift, ran it to the top of the shaft, then cut the rope. Instead of crashing to the floor, the elevator remained in place, held by the safety device he had designed.

Word of the safety elevator spread quickly,

and a few orders came in, but the American people were not yet ready to place their own lives on the line. All of the elevators sold in the first four years of business were used for freight.

The tide turned when an adventuresome businessman named E. V. Haughwort placed an order for a passenger elevator to serve the five floors of his New York department store. The elevator that Otis built for him traveled at the rate of forty feet a minute and cost three hundred dollars. It became an immediate hit with the store's customers.

As orders increased, so did the height of new buildings which "soared" to twelve or more floors. But even in his wildest dreams, Elisha Otis never imagined the heights to which his safety elevator would one day go.

One of the oldest Otis elevators still in operation today carries tourists from all over the world to the top of the Eiffel Tower in the center of Paris, France.

★ Levi Strauss
(Levi's Jeans)

Levi Strauss was born in Bavaria in 1829. When his father died, Levi's mother and her children moved to the United States to join the two oldest Strauss sons, who already had a dry-goods business in New York City. Eighteen-year-old Levi went to work for his stepbrothers but found it difficult to keep his mind on such mundane

things as bolts of cloth when he was hearing about
the discovery of gold in California.

In 1850, the young adventurer boarded a
clipper ship in New York harbor and set sail on
a rough seventeen-thousand-mile voyage that
would take him around South America to the
rowdy frontier town of San Francisco. To support
himself until he could strike gold, Levi's brothers
supplied him with generous samples of their stock
to sell—silks, broadcloths, and fine dress materials, as well as heavy canvas for tents and covers
for Conestoga wagons.

Strauss managed to sell all of the finer merchandise to the other passengers on the ship.
When he landed in San Francisco, he only had
the rough canvas left, but he was confident that
the prospectors would welcome some good,
sturdy material for tents.

Lugging his rolls of canvas through the gold-
rich hills of California, one old prospector looked
at the material and said: "Should'a brought pants.
Pants don't wear worth a hoot up in the diggin's!"

These words did not discourage Levi Strauss.
Instead, he found a tailor and asked him to make
up a pair of work pants using the heavy brown
canvas. The old prospector, according to the
story, was delighted with the durable pants and
told everybody about "those pants of Levi's."

Strauss had more heavy-duty pants made until he had used up his supply of canvas. He wrote
to his brothers and asked them to send more
heavy-duty material. They had run out of canvas,
so they sent him a heavy cotton fabric made in
France and called *serge de Nimes* (cloth from

Nimes). The name was later shortened to "de Nimes" and finally "denim." The term "jeans" was derived from a similar cloth made in the Italian city of Genoa.

Denim was softer than canvas, but just as strong. The neutral-colored material was dyed dark blue to hide soil stains. With production in full swing, the firm of Levi Strauss and Company was officially formed in 1853, and Levi's two brothers joined him as partners.

The use of copper rivets at the corners of pockets and other tension points was not Levi Strauss's idea. It was suggested by a tailor in Carson City, Nevada, named Jacob W. Davis. Some miners had complained that the weight of gold nuggets caused their pockets to rip. As a joke, Davis took a pair of pants to a harness maker and asked him to rivet the corners of the pockets. To his surprise, the prospectors were pleased.

Davis wrote to Levi Strauss, offering to sell him a half interest in his innovative idea for sixty-eight dollars, which was the cost of a patent application. Strauss jumped at the opportunity. From that time on, rivets were an important part of every pair of Levi's pants.

For over one hundred forty years, Levi's jeans have remained virtually unchanged despite many fashion trends, a claim that very few manufacturers can make.

★ George Westinghouse
(Westinghouse Electric Corp.)

Thomas Edison will forever be remembered as the inventor of the electric light. But it was George Westinghouse who figured out a way to transmit electricity over long distances to light those electric bulbs.

You'll find Westinghouse's name on many light bulbs and household appliances today, but it was the air brake and other safety devices for railroads that first brought this inventive genius to public attention over a century ago. During his lifetime, he was awarded more than four hundred patents—this averaged out to one every six weeks during his working life!

George Westinghouse was the son of a successful manufacturer of agricultural machinery in upstate New York. He would often play hooky from school and hide in corners just to watch his father's employees working on the machines. He was fascinated with anything mechanical.

In 1861, when he was only fifteen years old, George invented a rotary steam engine. When the Civil War broke out that same year, he joined the Union Army as an assistant engineer. When the war was over, he attended Union College briefly and then went to work for his father.

Westinghouse's first major achievement, and the one that first brought him wealth, was a fail-safe braking system for trains. Up until that time, train accidents occurred frequently because the brakes on each car had to be applied manually by a team of brakemen who got a signal from the engineer. A train chugging along at thirty miles an hour could travel almost a mile before coming to a complete stop.

After some experimentation with steam, Westinghouse finally developed a dependable braking system using compressed air, and it was tested for the first time on a run from Pittsburgh to Steubenville. The train had just gotten up to speed when the engineer saw a horse-drawn wagon on the tracks no more than several hundred feet up ahead. He applied the air brakes immediately and brought the train to a stop just a few feet from the frightened horses.

This dramatic incident proved that locomotives could now safely travel at faster speeds, but better signaling and switching devices would be needed. These were soon developed by Westinghouse.

In December of 1880, the thirty-four-year-old inventor's life took a dramatic turn when he went to Menlo Park, New Jersey, to see the first demonstration of Thomas Edison's new electric light. On his way home, Westinghouse became excited about the possibilities of electric power, but the mechanical genius spotted a drawback. The transmission of direct current was limited to a radius of only two or three miles. If electrical power was to be a commercial success, Westinghouse reasoned, a way would have to be found to transmit high-tension current over lines that could stretch for many miles.

Westinghouse began to experiment with alternating current (AC). Edison stubbornly main-

tained that direct current was the only safe way
to bring electricity into homes and offices. What
ensued was a verbal war that lasted for ten years.
The controversy was finally resolved in 1892 when
Westinghouse Electric won out over Edison's
General Electric to light the city of Niagara Falls.

The following year, the Chicago World's Fair
announced that the fairgrounds would be lit by
250,000 electric lights. Once again, Westinghouse
and Edison competed for the giant contract.
Westinghouse purposely underbid his rival by
more than $1 million. He was willing to lose
money in exchange for the priceless publicity that
he knew the project would bring him.

George Westinghouse won many awards and
honors in his long and productive career, but
none gave him more satisfaction than the one he
received from the American Institute of Electric
Engineers in 1914, just two years before his death.
It was the Edison Medal.

Because of his service in the Civil War, Westinghouse was granted a military burial in Arling-
ton National Cemetery. Ironically, the inscription
on his gravestone simply reads: "Acting Third Assistant Engineer, 1864–1865."

★ James Dole
(Dole Pineapple)

Long before Hawaii became the fiftieth state and
jet airliners could make the trip from California
in a matter of hours, Hawaii was a remote group

of islands in the middle of the Pacific Ocean, which took days to reach by ship.

A young twenty-two-year-old named James Dole made the trip in 1899. He had just graduated from Harvard, and he wanted to start a coffee plantation on one of the islands. When he tasted a succulent local fruit, he bought some land and decided to grow pineapple instead.

Dole knew that pineapple would make a big hit back in the States, once Americans could taste this unknown fruit. When local farmers hard about his plans, they laughed at the "ignorance" of this college graduate. They knew that pineapple spoiled very quickly and would never survive the long voyage to markets on the mainland.

James Dole endured their ridicule, for he had a plan. Instead of shipping fresh pineapple, he would export the fruit as a canned product. In 1903, three years after he had arrived in the tropical paradise, he built a small cannery and sent almost two thousand cans to a food distributor in San Francisco. The exotic fruit became an instant hit with Americans.

It wasn't long before pineapples became one of the island's largest industries, and Dole's company accounted for over a third of all the pineapple shipped from Hawaii. The demand was drastically reduced when the Great Depression hit the United States.

The Hawaiian Pineapple Company underwent a complete reorganization in 1931 and James Dole, who had started it all, was forced out. Dole left his beloved islands and did not return until 1958, just five months before his death.

★ Maurice and Richard McDonald
(McDonald's Hamburgers)

The McDonald brothers were still in their twenties when they left their home in New Hampshire for California in 1930. Just as the forty-niners had headed west looking for gold almost a century before, Maurice and Richard McDonald were also hoping to strike it rich, or at least find work.

It was the beginning of the Great Depression. Back home, the big shoe factory in town had shut down and the boys' father had lost the only job he had ever had. California seemed like the place to go for a new start.

In Hollywood, Dick and Mac, as they were called, were both hired by a movie studio to push scenery around on the movie sets. The brothers thought there might be money in movies, so they opened a movie theater in nearby Glendale, but in four years of operation they never made enough money to pay the monthly rent of one hundred dollars.

A new phenomenon was developing in Southern California—the drive-in restaurant. The brothers opened a tiny drive-in in Pasadena. Dick and Mac cooked the hot dogs (not hamburgers) and mixed milkshakes while carhops served the customers sitting in their cars.

McDonald's drive-in became a teenage hangout. The parking lot was always crowded. Annual sales topped two hundred thousand dollars and the brothers split fifty thousand dollars in profits. With their new-found wealth, they bought a new car every year and moved into a ninety-thousand-dollar house.

In 1948, the brothers made a surprising move. They closed down the restaurant for three months and changed the business from a drive-in restaurant to a hamburger stand with a walk-up window. The old three-foot grill was replaced by two six-foot grills. Paper products took the place of plates and silverware. Carhops and dishwashers would no longer be needed.

The menu was also changed. There would be only nine items, and all of them would be pre-cooked and kept warm under heat lamps. The term "fast food" had not been coined yet, but the McDonalds were laying the foundation for a new industry. With these innovations, the price of a hamburger could be lowered from thirty cents to fifteen cents.

When the new stand opened, business was very slow. Even the old customers stayed away, and the brothers began to doubt the wisdom of what they had done. But they stuck it out, and business slowly began to grow. Because of the lower prices, the McDonalds were now beginning to attract more families, especially working-class families who could now afford to take their children out to dinner.

The success of their operation brought requests for franchises. The first went to a gasoline retailer named Neil Fox. The brothers worked with an architect to design the new store. It was Richard McDonald who came up with the idea of using golden arches.

Only fifteen franchises were sold in the next

couple of years. The brothers were not ambitious, and they could not spend all the money they were now making. "We were taking it easier," they explained, "and having a lot of fun doing what we wanted to do." McDonald's would never have become a nationwide corporation (today it is worldwide), if Ray Kroc had not come upon the scene.

Ray A. Kroc was a fifty-two-year-old salesman for a milkshake mixer company. One of the products he sold was the Prince Castle Multi-Mixer, a deluxe contraption that could mix six milkshakes simultaneously. The McDonald brothers had ordered eight of these machines and Kroc was curious as to why one eating establishment would need to make forty-eight milkshakes at one time.

In 1954, Kroc visited McDonald's hamburger stand in San Bernardino, California, to see for himself. He couldn't believe his eyes. Customers were lined up at the window to order ready-made hamburgers and french fries. They received their orders in a matter of minutes. Uniformity and speed seemed to be the key to the stand's success.

The next day, Ray Kroc approached the brothers with an offer to franchise their operation. Dick and Mac were not interested. They were satisfied with their business as it was and they didn't want it to get any bigger. Kroc persisted and the brothers finally gave in.

Kroc went to work immediately and began selling McDonald's franchises all over the country. By 1961, there were over three hundred successful McDonald's stores in operation. The only thing standing in the way of Ray Kroc's driving ambition were the two brothers who had started it all, so Kroc bought out Maurice and Richard McDonald for $2.7 million. Had they hung on, the brothers' could have earned more than $55 million a year in royalties. Why did they sell? They weren't sure if the fast-food business wasn't just a passing fad.

This "fad" now serves seven percent of the U.S. population every day. In one year, it is estimated that almost sixty percent of American consumers eat at least one meal in a McDonald's. In 1990, the corporation made world headlines when they opened their first fast-food store in Moscow. Soon the entire globe will be able to fit under the golden arches.

★ Wally Amos
(Famous Amos Cookies)

Is there anyone who doesn't like chocolate chip cookies? A walk down the cookie aisle of any supermarket will reveal that chocolate chip is the number one favorite with cookie lovers in America. One of the most tasty chocolate chip cookies sold today is the *Famous Amos* brand.

Wally Amos was born in 1936, and he was far from famous when he moved from Tallahassee, Florida, to live with his Aunt Della in New York City. She gave him lots of love, as well as cookies made from her special recipe that turned the boy into a chocolate chip cookie fanatic.

As soon as he was old enough, Wally dropped out of school and spent four years in the Air

Force. Back in civilian life, with a wife and two small children to support, he worked as a book-keeper in a department store for a modest salary.

Although the job offered some security for his family, Amos craved more excitement. After four years of tedious work, the energetic young man quit his job and went to work as a mail carrier for the William Morris Agency, the world's largest talent agency. Within a very short time, he became the first African-American agent to work at the agency, and his clients included the Temptations, the Supremes, Marvin Gaye, and Bobby Goldsboro. He also signed on Simon and Garfunkel, who were then unknown performers.

In 1967, Amos left the agency to manage a well-known trumpeter, but the two had serious differences of opinion and Wally Amos found himself without a job. It couldn't have happened at a worse time. His wife had recently given birth to their third child and the family had just moved to California.

It was a low point in Amos's life. To take his mind off his troubles, he spent hours in the kitchen baking chocolate chip cookies from his Aunt Della's recipe. His friends had never tasted cookies that rich and good and they thought he should go into the cookie business.

A few of his friends went further than making suggestions. The singer Marvin Gaye, United Artists Records president Artie Mogull, Helen Reddy and her husband, Jeff Wald, put up a substantial sum of money to help Wally Amos launch the business. In March of 1975, he opened a cookie store on Sunset Boulevard. Fifteen hundred people showed up for the gala event, which offered free champagne, valet parking, and a strolling band.

A production plant was opened in Nutley, New Jersey, and another one in Van Nuys, California, turning out over seven thousand pounds of cookies a day. In the first two years, the business grossed more than one million dollars each year.

It could be said that Wally Amos is one "smart cookie" who is really "in the chips."

★ Joyce C. Hall
(Hallmark Cards)

Growing up in a small Nebraska town near the turn of the century, young Joyce Clyde Hall had two strikes against him.

First, there was his given name. His mother had named her youngest son after a Methodist bishop she admired—Isaac W. Joyce. The feminine first name was to plague Hall the rest of his life. Since his middle name wasn't much better, he used the nickname J.C.

The second burden came when his father, a traveling preacher, abandoned the family. Nine-year-old Joyce helped out with a variety of odd jobs—selling lemonade to circus-goers, sandwiches to passengers on passing railroad trains, and perfume to neighbors and friends. At the age of sixteen, Joyce and his two older brothers, William and Rollie, pooled their resources and started a business selling imported postcards.

In the first decade of the 1900s, only wealthy people could afford the engraved Christmas cards and fancy Valentine cards that were available. Picture postcards were less expensive and could be used for any occasion. They soon became a fad.

In 1910, at the age of eighteen, Joyce Hall dropped out of high school, crammed two shoeboxes full of postcards and boarded a train for Kansas City, determined to start a mail-order business.

In his room at the local YMCA, Joyce made up packets of one hundred cards and mailed them out to dealers throughout the Midwest. Some kept the cards without paying. Some returned the merchandise with angry notes. But about a third sent checks. Within a few months, the young businessman had made a profit of two hundred dollars and opened a bank account.

Joyce's brother, Rollie, joined him in Kansas City and the two formed Hall Brothers, a name that would appear on the back of cards until the mid-fifties. At first, the brothers bought greeting cards that had been created and printed elsewhere and sold them wholesale. Then on a fateful January day in 1915, with a building full of Valentine cards ready to be shipped out, a fire destroyed the entire inventory and left the brothers seventeen thousand dollars in debt.

Joyce Hall refused to accept defeat. With a loan from a sympathetic banker who believed in the hardworking brothers, they not only rebuilt but bought an engraving company that had been one of their suppliers. Now they could begin to design and print their own cards.

One of the first cards that the Hall brothers produced carried a message that had a special meaning for them. "When you get to the end of your rope," it read, "tie a knot in it and hang on."

The Hall brothers—all three of them now—hung on and saw their greeting card company grow into the world's largest. Today, the company produces more than eleven million greeting cards each day, prints them in twenty languages, and distributes them in more than one hundred countries. To produce this enormous output, Hallmark employs the world's largest creative staff: seven hundred writers and artists.

From the very beginning, J.C. insisted on quality, and every new design had to be approved by him. His goal was to carry on the tradition of fourteenth-century English craftsmen who worked in long rooms called halls. Each hall competed with the others to turn out superior work, and each stamped its work with a symbol or mark called a "hallmark." J.C. put his "hallmark" on every product he turned out. In 1954, the company's name was changed to Hallmark and the symbol was a crown.

A creative vice president at Hallmark came up with the company's slogan: "When you care enough to send the very best." According to several independent research studies, it is the most believed advertising slogan in the United States.

In his autobiography, *When You Care Enough*, Joyce Hall wrote: "If a man goes into business with only the idea of making a lot of money, chances are he won't. But if he puts service and quality first, the money will take care of itself. Producing a first-class product that is a real need is a much stronger motivation for success than getting rich."

Hall put his words into action when, nearing the age of eighty, he decided to transform twenty-five run-down blocks of downtown Kansas City into a city-within-a-city to be known as Crown Center. The five-hundred-million-dollar development is probably the largest urban renewal project ever to be financed with private funds.

Joyce Hall, who died in 1982, cared enough to give *his* very best.

Left: Harvey S. Firestone, Sr., founded the Firestone Tire & Rubber Company.

Right: Herman Lay founded H. W. Lay Company, which would later become Frito-Lay®, Inc.

Left: With his brothers, George Swinnerton Parker formed Parker Brothers, the company known for the bestselling game Monopoly.

Above: Bill Hewlett (standing) and Dave Packard developed an innovative audio oscillator in their garage in 1939.

Above Left: William Wrigley, Jr., created America's favorite chewing gum.

Above Right: George Eastman, depicted in an 1877 cartoon, invented film, which would revolutionize the photography industry.

★

Above Left: Dr. Edwin H. Land startled the photography industry with his invention of the Polaroid camera.

Above Right: The Gerber Baby has surely become the most famous baby in the world.

★

Above Left: King Camp Gillette invented the disposable razor blade.

Above Right: Alfred C. Fuller made his brushes by hand in the early days of his business.

★

Above Left: F. W. Woolworth opened his first 5 and 10¢ Store in 1879.

Above Right: Elisha G. Otis demonstrating his new elevator.

★

Above Left: Wally Amos used his aunt's special recipe to make his cookies.

Above Right: Elizabeth Arden, a leader of the American cosmetics industry.

★

Above Left: Mary Kay Ash, founder of Mary Kay Cosmetics, Inc.

Above Right: Borden's Condensed Milk Co., now Borden, Inc., was located in New York from 1889 to 1903.

★

Richard W. Sears (above left) and Alvah C. Roebuck (above right) founded Sears, Roebuck and Co.

———★———
Left: Dwight Hamilton Baldwin founded the Baldwin Piano and Organ Company.

———★———
Right: Colonel Harland Sanders invented an American favorite— Kentucky Fried Chicken.

———★———
Left: Richard Samuel Reynolds founded the Reynolds Metals Company.

William Procter (above left) and James Gamble (above right) founded the Procter & Gamble Company, producers of Ivory Soap.

★

Above: Henry Ford sits behind the wheel of a 1903 Model A.

★

Top: J. L. Kraft began his business by selling cheese wholesale to local grocers.

Middle: H. J. Heinz's company is known for a wide variety of bottled food products.

Bottom: J. C. Penney's first store was called the Golden Rule Store.

★ 5 ★

Beauty Queens

The enterprising women who started the beauty revolution in the early 1900s had two difficult hurdles to overcome. First of all, it was considered improper and unbecoming for women to work for a living. Secondly, "nice" women did not wear makeup. At least, they didn't admit to it. There were some women, however, who were determined to change these notions, and they became leaders of the cosmetics industry.

★ Elizabeth Arden
(Elizabeth Arden Cosmetics)

The woman who is largely responsible for starting the cosmetics industry in the United States
was not a U.S. citizen but a young Canadian girl,
and Elizabeth Arden was not her real name.

The pioneer of scientific beauty treatment
was born around 1890 in Woodbridge, a small
town near Toronto, the daughter of a Scottish
father who had come to Canada with his English
bride. The youngest of five children, she was given
the name Florence Nightingale Graham. When
the little girl was only five years old, her mother
died.

To no one's surprise, young Florence Nightingale left school before she was eighteen and
went into nurses' training. But she tired of it after
only a few weeks. Later on in life, she explained
that she didn't only want to make people well, she
also wanted to make them beautiful.

In 1909, the young Canadian arrived in New
York City. She got a secretarial job in the offices
of a London cosmetics firm, but found herself
more interested in the beauty treatments that
were given in the salon than in operating a type-
writer. She soon discovered that she had "won-
derfully magnetic hands for massage" and it
wasn't long before she was in demand for her
expert facial treatments. Her employers rewarded
her by teaching her the basic formulas for making creams and lotions.

With this valuable knowledge, Graham went

into partnership with a friend and opened a shop on Fifth Avenue. But the two friends soon discovered that they were not compatible business partners, and the shop folded within a year.

Graham thought it was time to strike out on her own, and borrowing six thousand dollars from a cousin, she opened a salon on Fifth Avenue. With the new salon and her expert beauty treatments, Florence Nightingale Graham hoped to attract the upper class of New York society. But her name didn't seem to match the elegant surroundings. After some thought, she came up with the name Elizabeth Arden, taking it from two of her favorite literary works—"Elizabeth and Her Garden" and Tennyson's poem "Enoch Arden."

Women flocked to her salon for her massage treatments, but she soon began to formulate a whole line of skin creams. Then, as more women began to wear makeup, she came out with a complete line of cosmetics that began to sell in department stores around the country. Her famous salon on Fifth Avenue, with its lacquered red door and uniformed doorman, continues to attract women who can afford to pamper themselves and have Elizabeth Arden make them more beautiful.

★ Mary Kay Ash
(Mary Kay Cosmetics)

If you see a pink Cadillac on a street in your hometown, chances are the owner is a woman who was awarded the automobile for being one of the top sales directors of Mary Kay Cosmetics. Mary Kay Ash has been giving away pink Cadillacs to her top money-makers for years. But when she started her business just a little over twenty-five years ago, the woman from Houston wasn't sure her company would even get off the ground.

When Mary Kay was only seven years old, she was given the responsibility of taking care of her invalid father who had spent three years in a sanitarium for tuberculosis. The awesome task would have challenged most children twice her age, but Mary Kay's mother had faith in her daughter and continually told her she was capable of the task. Mary Kay's mother worked fourteen hours a day managing a restaurant in Houston. She had to leave home every morning before Mary Kay got up and would often not return until long after the exhausted little girl had gone to bed.

For Mary Kay, there was no time for fun and games. As soon as she came home from school, she had to clean the house, take care of her father's needs, and then cook supper. Even as a seven-year-old, Mary Kay became quite a good cook, although she would occasionally have to call her mother at work when her father asked for something she didn't know how to prepare.

When she needed new clothes, Mary Kay would get some money from her mother and take the streetcar downtown on a Saturday morning. She would pick out a dress she liked and pay for it, much to the astonishment of salesclerks, who wondered where the little girl's mother was.

Mary Kay eventually grew up, got married, had three children, and worked twenty-five years in direct sales. When it was time to retire, Mary Kay began to think seriously about her "dream company"—a sales business of her own where she could give women all across the country the opportunity to gain self-confidence and earn money without neglecting their home and family responsibilities.

Once again her mother's words of encouragement rang in her ears. All she needed was a product for women to sell. Then she remembered the beauty products she had been using for years.

She had been introduced to the creams and lotions by a woman whose father had been a tanner of leather. He had noticed that as he treated the rough, porous hides to make them as smooth as glove leather, his hands became soft and youthful-looking while his face remained old and cracked. His daughter (Mary Kay's friend) modified the creams, used them on her hands and face, and saw remarkable improvements. The daughter moved to Dallas to study cosmetology and bottled her creams and lotions to sell to friends, but never tried to go into business.

Mary Kay realized she now had the products that would turn her dream business into a reality. She bought the formulas from her friend and began to manufacture them under her own name.

Mary Kay's plan was to select a group of women and train them in the proper use of the skin creams so they could demonstrate on prospective clients. These sales representatives would not be employed by Mary Kay, but would be independent businesswomen who would buy the products at wholesale prices and sell them at retail.

One month before the new company was to be launched, Mary Kay's husband died suddenly of a heart attack. Mary Kay was devastated and didn't think she could start a new business without her husband to guide her. Although her lawyer and accountant both told her to sell the company and get out before she lost everything, her three children urged her to go ahead.

Her twenty-nine-year-old son, Richard, offered to quit his good job with the Prudential Life Insurance Company and become the manager of the new business at a big cut in salary. His older brother, Ben, had a wife and two children to support. It would take him a little longer to make the move, but he gave his mother his life savings of forty-five hundred dollars. Daughter Marylyn later joined the business as the first Mary Kay sales director in Houston.

On September 13, 1963, one month after her husband's funeral, Mary Kay Cosmetics opened its doors as a small company in Texas. It wasn't long before Mary Kay had trained sales representatives all over the country; now, they are in many parts of the world. Thousands of confident women—many who had never worked before—became successful sales directors. Their lives were turned around because a dynamic woman in Dallas, Texas, told them, "You can do it!"

★ Estée Lauder
(Estée Lauder Cosmetics)

In 1978, when Princess Diana was in the United States, she wanted three people to be invited to a White House dinner in her honor: Bruce Springsteen, Robert Redford, and Estée Lauder. That was quite an honor for the daughter of Hungarian-Czech immigrants who grew up in Queens, New York.

The name on her birth certificate was Josephine Esther Mentzer, although her father had wanted to call her "Esty." Her middle name was later changed to Estée. (The accent mark was added by a schoolteacher who thought it would give the name a French flavor.)

Shortly after World War I broke out, her mother's brother came from Hungary to live with the family. John Schotz was a chemist who specialized in skin-care preparations, and he set up a makeshift laboratory in a tiny stable behind the Mentzer house. The young girl watched with fascination as her uncle mixed up his secret formula and filled small jars with the magic cream that made one's face feel as smooth as silk. Estée tried the preparation on all her friends at high school. "I didn't have a single friend," she said later, "who wasn't slathered in our creams."

After she married her first beau, Joe Lauder, Estée asked her uncle if she could put her new name on the labels of his facial creams and try to sell them around New York City. He agreed.

Estée Lauder went from salon to salon, set-

ting up a counter in one corner of each store.
While customers sat under the dryers with nothing to do, she would apply her creams free of
charge. After each treatment, the grateful customer usually left with an armful of Estée Lauder
products and a free sample of a product she
hadn't bought.

One of the keys to Estée Lauder's success was
that she always gave a gift with every purchase.
The free sample, she reasoned, was the best ad-
vertisement for her products and usually resulted
in future sales.

As the popularity of these quality products
began to spread, Lauder knew she needed help.
She couldn't be everywhere at once. As it was, she
was working every day from nine in the morning
until six in the evening. She never stopped for
lunch. An ad in the local newspaper brought in
twenty young women who were trained to be
demonstrator-salespeople.

Estée Lauder launched her company in 1946
with four products. By 1960, sales had gone over
one million dollars. Today, Estée Lauder, Inc., is
the third largest cosmetics and perfume firm in
the country, with annual sales estimated at over
one billion dollars.

★ Helena Rubinstein
(Helena Rubinstein Cosmetics)

Life magazine once called her "perhaps the
world's most successful businesswoman." During

the first forty-five years of her cosmetics business, Helena Rubinstein made more than twenty-five million dollars. At one time, she had homes in Paris, London, New York, and Connecticut. All of this came from the little jars of creams and lotions that she sold at fancy prices.

Helena Rubinstein was born in Krakow, Poland, in 1882. She was one of eight daughters in a middle-class Jewish family. Her father was a merchant.

In 1902, at the age of twenty, Rubinstein did an adventurous thing. She set sail halfway around the world to visit relatives in Melbourne, Australia. As soon as she arrived, she noticed that many of the women had dry, weather-beaten skin because of the incessant sun and heat. Her own skin was soft and white, thanks to a special cold cream she had been using in Poland since she was a young girl.

She had brought a supply of the cream with her, but soon gave it away to her friends. She wrote her mother to send a big supply of the facial cream and opened a shop in Melbourne to sell the product to the local women. She added a few other items for the skin and hair and became an instant success.

A year and a half later, the twenty-two-year-old left the Melbourne store in the hands of her sister and sailed for Europe to start a business there.

If she was going to advise women on the care of their skin and create better products to do the job, she felt she needed to know more about human skin from a medical point of view. She studied dermatology with some of the finest doctors in Vienna, Berlin, Munich, and Paris. In 1908, she opened a shop in London, but everyone told her she was doomed to fail. In those days, even lipstick was not worn by "nice" ladies in England.

Helena Rubinstein was not one to accept defeat. She converted a house owned by Lord Salisbury into a beauty salon and fitted it with expensive equipment. It wasn't long before fashionable ladies from London society and noblewomen from the Continent, including a number of princesses, came knocking on her door.

Helena Rubinstein soon opened salons in Paris, New York, Chicago, Boston, and Los Angeles. Then she packaged her products to be sold in department stores.

With her black hair pulled straight back into a bun, the elegant Madame Rubinstein turned heads wherever she went. She was also tireless. She was in her office, working, just two days before she died in 1965 at the age of ninety-four.

★ 6 ★

In the Right Place
at the Right Time

Being in the right place at the right time has led to more discoveries and business successes than most people are willing to admit. Good timing, however, can only *open* the door to opportunity when it knocks. Native ability, ingenuity, adaptability, a keen sense of salesmanship, and just plain hard work are necessary to turn opportunities into financial rewards.

★ Clarence Birdseye
(Birds Eye Frozen Foods)

People were always asking Clarence Birdseye about his unusual last name. He never got tired of giving an explanation because it was one of his favorite stories.

One of his ancestors had been a page in the royal court of England in the days when a person might be identified by a physical characteristic, an occupation, or a particular accomplishment. One day, while accompanying the queen on a hunting trip, Birdseye's ancestor saw a hawk circle above and dive toward the royal head. The quick-thinking page shot the hawk right through the eye with an arrow. From that moment on, he was called "Birds Eye" by the grateful queen.

His name was not the only unusual thing about Clarence Birdseye. He also had an unlikely background for a person who wanted to be a naturalist and adventurer. He was born in Brooklyn, New York, in 1886 to a well-to-do family, and his father was a wealthy Connecticut inventor. Bob (as he was called by all who knew him) later moved to Gloucester, Massachusetts, and was educated at Amherst College.

After graduating, Birdseye moved to Labrador, where he worked a variety of jobs: trapper, fur trader, fisheries investigator, biologist, and purchasing agent. During the bitter cold of the arctic winters, when the temperature would get down as far as fifty degrees below zero, he would watch as the Eskimos spread their freshly caught fish on the snow. Almost instantly, the fish were frozen solid. Months later, when a fish was thawed and cooked, it tasted as if it had been freshly caught. The same results were achieved with freshly killed caribou and geese.

Birdseye had eaten food that had been frozen in the conventional way—at a slower rate and at a higher than subzero temperature—and he was well aware of the tasteless results. The secret of locking in freshness, he concluded, was rapid freezing.

In 1923, when Birdseye was taking inventory of his life and trying to find direction and purpose, he remembered observing nature's "secret" of preserving food and retaining its freshness. He decided to work on this concept to see what he could do with it.

Birdseye consulted nutritionists who agreed that fast freezing of foods at subzero temperatures could lock in flavor and preserve basic nutrients. They told him that he had a great idea—*if* he could find a practical way to make it work.

That was all the encouragement the forty-year-old Birdseye needed. He borrowed on his life insurance policy and began experiments. Although he had no formal technical training, he designed and built a device that he called a "belt froster." He persuaded three investors to put up sixty thousand dollars, and General Seafoods Corporation was organized in 1923.

Birdseye's experiments continued. The first floor of the company's two-story building in Gloucester was a laboratory for experiments with all types of food. Unfortunately, Americans did not share Clarence Birdseye's enthusiasm for frozen food. In fact, resistance came from two fronts. Store owners did not want to spend money for special refrigeration equipment, and consumers turned a cold shoulder to what they saw was just another "cold storage" product.

Birdseye's company was about to go under when the Postum organization (makers of *Grape-Nuts* and *Postum*) came along and bought the assets of General Seafoods Corporation for twenty-two million dollars. The name of the company was changed to General Foods, which today is a giant in the food industry.

The new corporation went to work in a big way. Birdseye was named head of the General Foods laboratory in Gloucester, Massachusetts. The management selected eighteen grocery stores in Springfield, Massachusetts, and installed, free of charge, specially designed storage cases at a cost of fifteen hundred dollars each. A team of demonstrators offered shoppers free samples of chicken, haddock, sirloin steak, and strawberries. Speakers employed by the new company appeared before domestic science classes and women's clubs. A strong advertising campaign ran for forty weeks. Birds Eye Frozen Foods was on its way, slowly but surely, to becoming a multimillion-dollar corporation, all because one man happened to be in the right place to observe what the Eskimos had known for centuries—that quick-freezing is a natural process of preservation.

IN THE RIGHT PLACE AT THE RIGHT TIME   93

★ C. W. Post
(Post Cereals)

Charles William Post did not look like a successful businessman when he came to Dr. John
Kellogg's famous sanitarium in Battle Creek,
Michigan. He had suffered a number of setbacks
in business and, although he was only thirty-
seven, he was so weak that he had to be pushed
around in a wheelchair by his wife.

Dr. Kellogg served no meat, coffee, or tea at
his sanitarium, which was owned by the Seventh-
Day Adventist Church. He believed that proper
foods could cure most illnesses, and to make
meals at the sanitarium more palatable, Dr. Kellogg and his younger brother, Will, began experiments to create new foods. After many false
starts, the brothers finally came up with toasted
flakes made from corn and a coffee substitute derived from cereal grains. We don't know if these
"health foods" worked or not. According to one
writer, Charles Post was discouraged that he could
not be cured of his many vague illnesses. One
day, he just got up from his wheelchair and left
the sanitarium.

Post stayed in Battle Creek and started a
business in a barn where he began to make a cereal beverage of his own. He called his drink
Monk's Brew, and advertised the drink as a
"builder of red blood." A year later, in 1896, he
changed the name to *Postum*.

Two years later, Post introduced one of the
first ready-to-eat cold cereals. It was made of

baked wheat and malted barley and resembled the granola that had been served at Kellogg's sanitarium. He called the new product *Grape-Nuts*, although it contained neither grapes nor nuts. Post mistakenly believed that grape sugar was formed during the baking operation, and the cereal did have a nutty taste.

Like Postum, the new cereal was also sold as a health food, and it gave Charles Post a healthy income. By 1901, Postum and Grape-Nuts were bringing in close to $1 million a year.

In 1904, two years before Will Kellogg started his own company to make the corn flakes that he and his brother had developed, Charles Post came out with his own version. Being a religious man, he named his new product *Elijah's Manna*, but he soon discovered that he had made a mistake. Ministers across the country were denouncing Post from their pulpits for using a biblical name to sell corn flakes. It wasn't long before the name was changed to *Post Toasties*.

★ Gail Borden
(Borden Milk)

Gail Borden led a colorful life before he entered the dairy business in his early fifties. He was born in 1801 in Norwich, New York. His father was a farmer; his mother, a great-great-granddaughter of Roger Williams, who established Rhode Island and founded the first Baptist church in America. His family became part of the first great wave of westward migration in 1815, settling first in Kentucky and then in Indiana.

By the time he reached the age of twenty, young Gail had been a schoolteacher for two years, even though he may only have had a year and a half of formal schooling. But Gail and his younger brother, Tom, were not ready to settle down. They jumped at the chance to take a flatboat down the Mississippi River with supplies for the settlers who had migrated to New Orleans. Once there, they heard the exciting news that the vast territory of Texas was being opened to settlers.

Tom joined Stephen F. Austin's pioneer band of three hundred families. Because of ill health, Gail had to stay behind, and he moved to Mississippi, where he spent the next six years teaching school and surveying. During this time, he married a sixteen-year-old girl named Penelope Mercer.

In 1829, in response to his brother Tom's enthusiastic letters about "the promised land," Gail and his wife set out for the Texas territory. He was granted over four hundred acres of land along the Colorado River to farm and raise cattle. When war with Mexico broke out, Borden became editor of the rebels' newspaper, the *Telegraph and Texas Land Register*. On April 21, 1836, he headlined Colonel Sydney Sherman's historic words, "Remember the Alamo!" helping to make them the battle cry that inspired the new republic.

When the war was over, the president of the Republic of Texas, Sam Houston, rewarded Gail

Borden by appointing him tax collector for the Port of Galveston. The title sounded important, but the pay was very meager, and with a wife and six children to support, Borden needed to augment his income. He started thinking more about an idea he had long nurtured—that food could be preserved and made safer by condensation. When his beloved wife and four-year-old son died in a yellow fever epidemic in 1844, and another son died two years later, Borden's work almost became an obsession.

With no refrigeration and a nation on the move, a way to preserve food for long periods of time was long overdue. Borden first experimented with meat and soon came up with a product that he called "meat biscuits." A party of forty-niners took his biscuits to California during the gold rush, and the American explorer, Dr. Elisha Kent Kane, used some on one of his Arctic expeditions.

After five years of struggle, Borden's money was almost gone as he tried to sell his meat biscuits to a reluctant public and an uninterested Army and Navy. But in 1851, his new product was awarded the Great Council Medal at the International Exhibition in London. It was on his trip back from accepting the award that circumstance played an important role in Gail Borden's life.

During the long ocean crossing, he heard the anguished cries of sick babies and saw several distraught mothers holding infants in their arms who were dying because of impure milk from two unhealthy cows kept in the hold of the steamer. That image would to haunt him for years.

Borden had tried unsuccessfully to condense milk during the first years of his experiments in Galveston. Now he was determined to try again. In two years' time, he found the answer that had long baffled scientists.

He boiled off the water, which makes up over eighty-seven percent of milk, in airtight vacuum pans. From beginning to end, his process excluded air. The result was a safe product that kept well for long periods of time.

In Washington, however, his patent application was denied. The patent commissioner ruled that there was "nothing new" in Borden's process. The verdict came as a stunning blow to Borden. He was deeply in debt from the failure of his meat biscuits, and to prove his right to a milk-condensing patent would take money and time.

Two distinguished scientists came to Borden's rescue. One was Robert McFarlane, editor of *Scientific American*. The other was Dr. John H. Currie, head of a major research laboratory. They tested every known method of condensing milk and presented evidence that Borden's process was not only different, but superior. The three-year battle with the patent office ended on August 19, 1836, when Gail Borden, now fifty-four, was finally granted a patent.

The legal battles were over, but financial problems once again took over. Borden opened a small plant in Wolcottville, Connecticut, with the help of a wealthy Washington lawyer. Within a few months, however, the venture failed. It was underfinanced, local farmers refused to extend credit for fresh milk, and the trickle of condensed milk that reached New York City was met with negative reactions from housewives who were used to the products manufactured by other dairies.

His original backer agreed to finance a second try, and Borden opened a new plant in Burrville, Connecticut. Unfortunately, the financial panic of 1857 had just hit and the second plant seemed doomed to failure.

Once again, circumstance stepped in to save Gail Borden and the product that was destined to revolutionize the dairy industry.

During a train trip to New York from his Connecticut plant, Borden started talking to the stranger who sat next to him. He began to tell him about his dreams and the financial obstacles that were standing in his way. The man that he just happened to sit next to turned out to be Jeremiah Milbank, a banker and wholesale grocer. When the train arrived at its destination, the two men shook hands and a new partnership was formed. Milbank agreed to pay off Borden's debts and manage his finances. The New York Condensed Milk Company—later to become the Borden Company—was on its way, and production at the Burrville plant went into full operation.

After years of struggle, Gail Borden was due for some good luck, and it came in two very different events. First was a campaign launched by a popular New York newspaper against distillery milk, which was the only kind of milk available to city dwellers at the time. The newspaper praised the purity of Borden's milk, with the result that sales began to rise.

The other event was the beginning of the

Civil War. The struggling company, less than two years old, received its first government order for five hundred pounds of condensed milk in the fall of 1861. From then on, Borden's problem was not sales, but how to increase production. *Eagle Brand Condensed Milk*, as the product was named, became part of the Union Army's field ration.

Civilian sales got a boost when Mrs. Lincoln served condensed milk at a White House dinner. When the Union soldiers returned home after the war, they told their wives about the "canned milk" they had consumed, and sales figures rose even higher.

What pleased Gail Borden more than the monetary rewards he was enjoying was the fact that those who used condensed milk were healthier than those who drank raw milk. Borden's process pasteurized the milk, though the fact that heating milk to 190 degrees destroys harmful bacteria wasn't scientifically proven until 1864 when Louis Pasteur made this discovery.

As his health failed, Gail Borden returned to Texas. The great failure of his life—the meat biscuit—somehow made his other accomplishments a little less satisfying. He built a small meat-preserving plant and put one of his sons in charge of it. The little town that grew up around the plant is still known as Borden, Texas, today. It was there that Gail Borden died on January 11, 1874, at the age of seventy-two.

His burial site, however, is Woodlawn Cemetery, just north of New York City. On a shady hillside overlooking the burial ground sits a monument with these simple words that summarize his life and struggles: "I tried and failed. I tried again and again, and succeeded!"

★ Robert Augustus Chesebrough
(Vaseline Petroleum Jelly)

In 1859, a retired railroad conductor named Edwin Drake drilled the world's first commercial oil well in Titusville, Pennsylvania, and the first oil boom was on.

At the time, Robert Chesebrough was a struggling twenty-two-year-old chemist who owned a small kerosene business. With natural petroleum available and cheaper, Chesebrough knew that kerosene would soon be on its way out. There was only one thing to do—get into the petroleum business without delay. He used his entire savings to buy a round-trip train ticket to Titusville.

Once there, Chesebrough didn't know what to look for. He roamed the oil fields, carefully observing every phase of the complex operations. His chemist's curiosity was aroused by a substance the workers called "rod-wax," a colorless oil residue that formed around the drilling rods. It intrigued him that the oil men cursed the pasty material when it gummed up their pumps but praised it when they cut or burned themselves and applied the paraffin-like substance to their wounds.

Chesebrough returned to Brooklyn, New York, with jars of the mysterious waste product and began months of experiments to extract and purify the paste's essential ingredient. The compound turned out to be a clear, smooth substance that he called *"Vaseline Petroleum Jelly."*

To test its healing qualities, Chesebrough inflicted cuts, scratches, and burns on his hands and arms. When he covered the injured areas with the paste, they healed quickly and without infection, though he would carry the scars from his experiments for the rest of his life.

By 1870, Robert Chesebrough had raised enough money to build a plant to manufacture his new preparation. He sent hundreds of samples to doctors, pharmacists, and scientific societies and waited for the orders to come in. When nothing happened, he hitched up his horse and buggy and headed for upstate New York, where he handed out free samples to every person he saw. The public's response was so favorable that within six months, Chesebrough had hired twelve salesmen to sell the jelly for a penny an ounce.

Chesebrough was surprised and pleased to learn that his customers were finding many practical uses for Vaseline. Housewives claimed that the jelly removed stains and rings from wood furniture and that it gave luster to leather goods. Farmers discovered that a coating of Vaseline on outdoor machinery prevented rusting. Druggists used the pure ointment as a base for their own brands of salves, creams, and cosmetics.

So great was Chesebrough's faith in his product that he swallowed a spoonful of it every day of his life, claiming in later years that it was the secret of his long life.

When he was in his late fifties, Chesebrough

was stricken with pleurisy. He instructed his nurse to give him a rubdown with Vaseline every day. Later, he joked that the jelly had caused him to "slip from death's grip."

No one has ever disputed Chesebrough's personal claim for his product. He lived until the ripe old age of ninety-six, and was active until the very end.

★ Ole Evinrude
(Evinrude Outboard Motors)

It was a hot summer day in 1904, according to the story, when Ole Evinrude took a neighbor named Bessie Cary on a picnic. The spot he picked was a small island in Lake Michigan. Everything went well until Bessie got a craving for some ice cream. Wanting to impress his date, the young man offered to row the two and a half miles back to shore to get some.

By the time Ole had rowed all the way back, the blazing sun had done its work and the ice cream had melted to a gooey mess. That embarrassing experience was the turning point in Evinrude's life. He resolved then and there to find an easier and faster way to propel a small boat through water. Five years later, Evinrude patented his revolutionary outboard motor and formed the Evinrude Motor Company to manufacture it.

From then on, the industrious mechanic had little time for picnics. The new company was swamped with orders for the dependable one-cylinder engine. Outboard motors buzzed across the nation's lakes like bees in a summer garden.

Much of the credit for the success of the business in those early days must go to the business manager and advertising director of the growing firm—the talented and hardworking woman named Bessie Cary Evinrude.

Obviously impressed by his chivalry, the neighborhood girl with the craving for ice cream had married Ole Evinrude soon after that fateful picnic.

★ Charles E. Hires
(Hires Root Beer)

Charles Hires was a young Philadelphia pharmacist who opened his own drugstore, borrowing three hundred dollars to outfit it with the latest fixtures, including a soda fountain made of marble.

Early in the 1870s, Hires married and spent his honeymoon on a New Jersey farm. While there, he was introduced to an exciting new drink made by the farmer's wife from sixteen different wild roots and berries. This "herb tea," as it was called, was already very popular in rural areas. Hires thought that city dwellers would enjoy the drink as well, so when he and his bride returned to Philadelphia, he had the recipe in his pocket.

Hires began experimenting with the drink in his drugstore and soon had samples made for tasting. One of the first to try the new concoction was a friend, Dr. Russell Conwell, the founder of Temple University. He agreed that this was a totally new taste, but suggested that more people—especially hard-drinking Pennsylvania coal miners—would be more likely to try it if it had a more appealing name than Hires Herb Tea. He suggested the name *Hires Root Beer*.

Hires Root Beer Extract was first introduced to the public at the Philadelphia Centennial Exposition in 1876. The extract was sold in twenty-five-cent packages. All a person had to do was add five gallons of water, four pounds of sugar, and half a yeast cake to make a refreshing drink at a cost of only five cents a gallon.

Soft drinks were rapidly becoming a national habit, but up until this time, no single drink had won more than local popularity. Charles Hires set out to change that with an advertising campaign and nationwide distribution. He became one of the very first national advertisers.

In 1893, bottled root beer—already mixed and ready to drink—went on the market. It was then that Hires ran up against the Women's Christian Temperance Union. The ladies of this organization could not believe that a drink with the word "beer" in its name could be nonalcoholic.

It is ironic that root beer had originally been promoted as a "temperance drink" and as a tonic to "purify the blood and make rosy cheeks." Being a Quaker, Hires had always been concerned about his product's mildness and the purity of its ingredients. He even refused to add caffeine to his drink.

The battle with the ladies of the WCTU raged in the newspapers for several years until Hires published the findings of an independent laboratory that confirmed the drink was nonalcoholic.

The Hires family retained private ownership of the company until 1968, when it was bought by Consolidated Foods Corporation. It is still the largest root beer maker in the world.

★ Charles A. Pillsbury
(Pillsbury Flour)

Charles Pillsbury graduated from Dartmouth College in 1863. He majored in languages—three years of Greek and Latin, and a year of French and German, hardly the right preparation for the vocation he eventually selected. His other courses included civil engineering, physics, and chemistry.

According to a classmate, "He did not seek to attain high scholarship. . . . He was a good talker and kept the fact constantly in mind that he meant to be a successful 'businessman.'"

It is not clear why Charles decided to move to Minneapolis, except that his uncle, John Pillsbury, was one of the city's most successful and respected citizens. He was owner of a wholesale and retail hardware business and a prominent member of the state senate. Later, John Pillsbury was to become the first three-term governor of Minnesota and widely recognized as "Father of the University of Minnesota."

There is almost no indication why Charles decided to go into the flour-milling business, but he did happen to be in the right place at the right time. Conditions had become just right for a successful milling industry in Minneapolis. There was ample wheat production in the area, plenty of low-cost power (thanks to a nearby waterfall on the Mississippi River), and several newly built railroad lines.

Charles and his father, who had also moved to Minneapolis, bought a one-third interest in a local flour mill. Most people in town thought that the father and son had been sold a very unstable business. Everyone knew that Minneapolis flour could not compare to the more popular winter wheat milled in St. Louis, and of the numerous flour mills in Minneapolis, this particular one had been losing money almost steadily.

Most of his competitors felt sorry for young Pillsbury. But Charles Pillsbury surprised everyone. He immediately set about to learn everything he could about the business, dealing with farmers personally for their wheat and keeping his eye on the daily operation of the mill. He began to improve the milling process to increase the quality and value of the flour. As a first step, he hired his chief competitor's head miller. Along with him, he got an improved technique for separating bran from the hard wheat flour.

By the time the company was celebrating its thirtieth anniversary in 1889, the C. A. Pillsbury

Company had become the world's largest milling enterprise, with daily production reaching ten thousand barrels. Charles Pillsbury had become one of Minnesota's most prominent citizens. Following the example of his uncle, he also entered politics and served five terms in the state senate.

★ William and Andrew Smith
(Smith Brothers Cough Drops)

James Smith was a skilled carpenter and equally talented candymaker who had moved his family from Scotland to Quebec, Canada, where they lived for fifteen years. In 1847, Smith moved to Poughkeepsie, New York, and opened a restaurant. His two sons, William and Andrew, helped with the family business. William, the oldest, was known as the "candy boy," selling his father's candy up and down the streets of the city.

One day, according to legend, a roving peddler by the name of Sly Hawkins stopped at Smith's Dining Saloon. When he couldn't pay his restaurant bill, Hawkins offered the owner a formula for a cough remedy. James, knowing that coughs and colds were common during the long, harsh winters of the Hudson River Valley, saw the sales potential of medicinal candy and bought the recipe for five dollars.

Using his candymaking skills, Smith cooked up a quantity of the cough drops and put them on sale in his restaurant. William and Andrew helped their father mix the secret formula, then went out on the streets of Poughkeepsie to sell the "cough candy," as they called it.

By the end of that harsh winter, people up and down the Hudson River had heard about the effective cough remedy. Manufacturing moved from the restaurant's kitchen to a nearby building. The drops were soon advertised as "James Smith & Sons Compound of Wild Cherry Cough Candy for the Cure of Coughs, Colds, Hoarseness, Sore Throats, Whooping Cough, Asthma, etc. etc."

When their father died in 1866, the boys continued the business under the name *Smith Brothers*. With success, however, came a rash of imitators—everything from Schmitt Brothers to Smythe Sisters. There were even some who brazenly used the Smith Brothers name to sell their poor imitations of the real thing.

William and Andrew knew they had to do something to protect their good name *and* their income. They registered their portraits as a trademark and placed their pictures on the large glass bowls that were used to display the cough drops on store counters. To prevent counterfeiters from putting their drops in the jars, the brothers molded the initials SB into each drop.

In 1877, the Smiths came out with the first factory-filled candy package ever produced in the United States. On the front of the box were the two portraits, with the word "Trade" under William's picture and "Mark" under Andrew's likeness. Because of the way the two words were positioned, the two brothers were thereafter known by those names. They didn't seem to mind.

After all, the publicity only sold more cough drops. Over the years, the daily production increased from five pounds a day to five *tons*!

Although long gone, the Smith Brothers are one of the most recognizable of all the men and women who left their "brand" on America. Their likenesses have been reproduced on millions of packages of *Smith Brothers Cough Drops* manufactured in the nearly 140 years of its existence.

It seems ironic, though, that William and Andrew Smith owed their fame and fortune to a man who couldn't "cough up" the price of a restaurant meal!

★ Richard Sears and Alvah Roebuck
(Sears, Roebuck and Co.)

Richard Warren Sears was a farmer's son whose childhood hobby was answering mail-order ads, then trading the merchandise he received with other boys in his hometown of Spring Valley, Minnesota. His life was to change drastically at sixteen when his father died and he became the sole supporter of his mother and two sisters.

Young Sears learned telegraphy and soon became a freight agent at the Minneapolis and St. Louis railway station in North Redwood, Minnesota, for the modest salary of six dollars a week. The work was easy and he was able to make extra money on the side, which his employer encouraged him to do.

It wasn't long before the young man had built a thriving part-time business, shipping lumber and coal (the railroad gave him special rates) and selling the products to local farmers and Native Americans. He often traded the wood and coal for produce that he sold to other customers (again using his cut-rate shipping privileges). Sears was honing his shrewd trading skills, which had been apparent since childhood.

In his job as freight agent, Sears also learned the ins and outs of the mail-order business. He studied catalogs and was able to figure out the markup between wholesale and retail prices. Then, in 1886, at the age of twenty-three, Richard Sears was ready to snatch a "golden" opportunity that came in the form of a box of "yellow watches" which had been sent to a local jewelry store on consignment.

The store refused the shipment, claiming they had not ordered the watches. When Sears contacted the Chicago watch company to tell them the shipment was being returned, he was told he could have the watches for only twelve dollars each. The gold-filled pocket watches were very popular at the time and were selling for about twenty-five dollars in most stores. Sears accepted the offer, but he had no desire to go into the retail business. Instead, he contacted all the freight agents up and down the line and offered the timepieces for fourteen dollars each. They, in turn, could sell the watches and keep whatever profit they could make.

In no time, all the watches had been sold and Sears had realized a profit of two dollars on each. He ordered more watches and offered them to other agents. Within six months, he had made more than five thousand dollars—a sizable sum in those days. He could now give up his railroad job and go into the mail-order business full time.

He moved to Minneapolis and established the R. W. Sears Watch Company. He started writing newspaper ads and discovered another natural talent—copywriting. His persuasive ads, which ran mostly in farm publications, resulted in a steady stream of orders. Within a matter of months, Sears decided to move his business to Chicago, which offered a more central location and better shipping facilities.

The first thing he did was write some ads for the Chicago newspapers to let the residents know that the Sears Watch Company was open for business. Then Sears wrote a special ad that would change his life and increase his fortune. It ran in the April 1, 1887, issue of the *Chicago Daily News*:

WANTED—Watchmaker with reference who can furnish tools. State age, experience and salary required. ADDRESS T39, Daily News.

In a furnished room in Hammond, Indiana, another farm boy, by the name of Alvah Curtis Roebuck, read and reread the ad in the *Chicago Daily News*. He was a born tinkerer and, like Richard Sears, had also learned telegraphy and been self-supporting since the age of sixteen. He had learned to repair watches through a correspondence course and was now employed as a watch repairman. He liked his job, but was making only $3.50 a week plus room and board.

Unlike Richard Sears, Alvah was a cautious man who did not act impulsively. He carefully weighed the opportunities that this new job might offer him, then finally decided to take a chance and answer the ad. Two days later, Sears asked him to come to Chicago for an interview.

When he walked into the office on Dearborn Street, the tall and slender Roebuck had with him a sample of his best work. Sears examined the timepiece as if he knew what he was looking for. Finally, he put the watch down and said, "I don't know anything about watchmaking, but I presume this is good, otherwise you wouldn't have submitted it to me. You look all right. You may have the position."

Alvah Roebuck was not only an excellent repairman, he could also build watches from scratch. On several occasions, Sears was able to buy large quantities of surplus parts from manufacturers at a fraction of what they had cost to produce. These parts, often from different manufacturers, were assembled by Roebuck and sold at prices much lower than those available elsewhere. The business grew by leaps and bounds, and Alvah Roebuck became Richard Sears's most valuable employee.

Just a year after coming to Chicago, the restless Sears wanted to try something new. He sold the business to his partner. Alvah Roebuck, who was still more interested in repairing watches than running a business, owned all that Richard Sears had created.

After only a week, Sears had changed his mind. He asked if he could buy half the business back again. Roebuck readily agreed. Soon after the partners were back together again, they published a 52-page catalog still devoted mostly to watches. Other items were soon added to the mail-order business, and a year later, the catalog doubled in size. In 1893, it expanded to 322 pages. In September of that year, the corporate name was officially changed to Sears, Roebuck and Company.

Although Richard Sears was a promotional genius, he was a poor businessman. Orders were coming in at a healthy pace, but the company was not run well and was losing money.

Roebuck was growing tired and worried. He did not like the long working hours (often sixteen hours a day, seven days a week), and the pressures of the company's financial problems were getting to him. In August of 1895, Roebuck walked into Sears's office and announced that he was quitting. He accepted an offer of twenty-five thousand dollars for his half of the business. If he had hung on a few more years, the business would have been worth millions.

Two investors bought into the company after Roebuck left, but Sears could not get along with them. He sold his stock for ten million dollars and, in 1914, died at the age of fifty.

Alvah Roebuck died in 1948 at the ripe old age of eighty-four. Whenever he was asked if he regretted having sold out so early and for so little, he would smile and shake his head. "I didn't become a millionaire," he would say, "but I've led a long and happy life." Then he would add with a twinkle in his eye, "They're all dead . . . and I never felt better!"

★ 7 ★

Necessity Is the
Mother of Invention

If necessity is the mother of invention, then ingenuity must be the father. Being able to adapt and switch gears has saved many businesses from going under. It is also a good piece of advice for individuals. "If life hands you a lemon," a modern-day philosopher has said, "make lemonade."

Many inventions and new products came about because some people were forced into action by circumstances beyond their control. In this chapter you'll meet eight individuals who found creative ways to overcome impossible situations.

★ Milton Bradley
(Milton Bradley Games)

When Abraham Lincoln took a young girl's advice and grew a beard to cover his scrawny face, he did not realize that his decision would drive a young Massachusetts printer to within a "hairsbreadth" of bankruptcy. The hapless victim of Lincoln's new look was Milton Bradley.

After graduating from high school, Bradley worked for a draftsman and sold stationery on the side. With the money he managed to save, he enrolled at the Lawrence Scientific School in Cambridge, Massachusetts, and after completing a year and a half of the two-year course, he moved with his family to Springfield, Massachusettes.

Bradley became interested in lithography—the process of reproducing pictures and other material through the use of a specially prepared printing plate. He went to Providence, Rhode Island, to learn the process, then returned to Springfield, bought a printing press, and started his own lithography business.

Bradley's first important job was a portrait of a young lawyer named Abraham Lincoln who was running for the office of president of the United States on the new Republican Party ticket. The lithographic portrait was made from an original photograph taken at the nominating convention by a reporter from the local newspaper. Milton Bradley hoped that his portraits of Lincoln would sell well, especially in his hometown. He was counting, perhaps, on the fact that the presidential candidate came from another city named Springfield—Springfield, Illinois.

During the presidential campaign, Lincoln grew the beard that would make him famous. The beard, of course, also made Bradley's lithographic portrait of a clean-shaven Lincoln obsolete, and he ended up destroying several thousand prints.

The future seemed bleak for the twenty-four-year-old businessman. His press was idle and there were no new jobs coming in. A friend suggested that Bradley invent a board game and print it on his press.

The desperate printer took his friend's advice and came up with a parlor game that he called "The Checkered Game of Life." Players made points by landing on squares with positive virtues and values and avoiding squares that represented misconduct and misfortune. Bradley peddled the games himself, traveling throughout New England and New York State. In just one year, he sold forty-five thousand copies.

In 1864, the same year that Lincoln ran for a second term in the White House, the firm of Milton Bradley and Company was formed. In the years that followed, the board game pioneer added more games to his line, providing hours of pleasure for generations of Americans who did not have radio, television, or the phonograph for entertainment.

★ Joshua Lionel Cowen
(Lionel Trains)

Intelligent, curious, probing—if there ever was a born inventor, Joshua Cowen was one. As a small boy in the 1880s, he cared little for formal education, but was so inquisitive he cracked open the heads of his sisters' expensive porcelain dolls to find out what made their eyes move.

High school bored him, so he was allowed to enroll at Peter Cooper Institute, a highly respected technical school in New York City. He spent most of the time in the science lab, where he could tinker and experiment to his heart's content. He was fascinated with electricity and a new concept still being developed—storing electricity in batteries. While at school, he invented a battery-operated doorbell, but abandoned the idea when a shortsighted instructor told him that the public would not be interested.

After enrolling and dropping out of college several times, the young man went to work for a small electrical shop in midtown Manhattan. During his apprenticeship there, he claimed to have invented a dry-cell battery to replace the containers of sulfuric acid that could eat through flesh or fabric if spilled. "I couldn't make it last more than thirty days," he said later on, "so I let it slide."

It was not the last invention that Cowen "let slide" in order to get on to other things. Most of his family and friends would agree that Joshua Cowen was impulsive and impatient.

Cowen did manage to patent two inventions while he worked at the electrical shop: a battery-operated photographer's flash and electric explosive fuses. With the patents under his arm, Cowen quit his job and opened his own company to manufacture electrical novelties.

One of his first creations was a small electric fan that ran on two dry-cell batteries. The only problem was that if you stood more than a foot from the fan, you couldn't feel a thing.

Another invention of the Cowen Manufacturing Company was an "electric flower pot." A slender battery in a tube with a tiny light bulb at one end was stuck in the middle of a plant to illuminate the leaves. One of Cowen's employees, Conrad Hubert, talked his boss into selling him the rights to the flower pot.

When the novelty item didn't sell, Hubert reworked the shape of the light and received a patent for a "portable electric light"—the first flashlight. The convenient light caught on so quickly that Hubert started his own business, the Eveready Flashlight Company, and became a millionaire.

Once again, Cowen had let a potential winner slip by. He was a man with his own business, but no product to sell. He must have looked many times at the small motor that had powered his breezeless fan. The motor had worked fine. If there was only something else he could do with it.

One day, while passing by a toy store near his place of business, Cowen stopped to admire a tin locomotive sitting in the window along with many other toys. His inventive mind perked up. If only that locomotive could be made to move, go around and around on a circular track without having to be wound up every couple of turns, it would catch the attention of passersby.

Back at his shop he went to work on the idea. His intention was to create not a new toy, but a device to display merchandise. The toy-store owner was delighted with Cowen's creation and bought it for four dollars. The next day he asked Cowen for another battery-powered locomotive. A customer who had seen the locomotive in the window bought it.

Other stores heard about the battery-operated locomotives and wanted some to sell. It finally dawned on Cowen that he had inadvertently created a successful new product—electric toy trains.

Since that day in 1901, many generations of children (and their fathers) have spent countless hours playing with the electric trains that were named for their unwitting inventor—Joshua *Lionel* Cowen.

★ Joseph Campbell
(Campbell's Soups)

Joseph Campbell had been surrounded by fruits and vegetables from early childhood. His father was a successful fruit farmer in southern New Jersey, and even when Campbell moved away from the family farm as a young man, he couldn't get

away from produce. Campbell moved to Philadelphia where, for the next twenty-five years, he
worked at various jobs in the fruit and vegetable
industry.

At the age of fifty-two, Campbell decided to
make a change. He teamed up with Abraham Anderson, who had a successful canning business in
Camden, New Jersey, across the Delaware River
from Philadelphia.

Joseph Campbell had some definite ideas on
how things should be done and, although he was
new to the business, he soon became the domi-
nant partner. The conservative Anderson wanted
his business to grow slowly, but Campbell had
other ideas. The older Campbell got, the younger
his ideas became.

After seven years of bickering, Abraham Anderson had finally had enough. He told his partner to either sell his half of the partnership or
buy the whole company. He assumed that since
Campbell had bought into the business, he would
be the one to get out. He was wrong.

At age fifty-nine, Joseph Campbell took over
the canning company with all its equipment, plus
the recipes for jams, jellies, apple butter, mince-
meat, and the prized canned tomatoes for which
the company had just won a medal at the Centennial Exposition of 1876 in Philadelphia.

Abraham Anderson wanted to get back at his
former partner by becoming a competitor. With
the money he had made from the sale, he bought
an old factory and converted it to a cannery. He
added canned soups to the usual line of fruits
and vegetables.

Joseph Campbell decided to counter with his own line of soups, but not the bulky, waterfilled cans that others were selling. They were difficult to ship and inconvenient to use. The solution came by way of a fortunate coincidence.

Shortly after Anderson had left to start his own company, a wealthy investor named Arthur Dorrance had become Campbell's new partner. Dorrance had a nephew named John who had just finished his studies in Europe and received a Ph.D. in chemistry. The young man, who just happened to have a passion for gourmet soups, decided to spend a few months working in the kitchens of some of the top restaurants in Paris to discover how chefs made their world-famous soups.

Young John Dorrance returned to America and got a job with his uncle's canning company (Arthur Dorrance was now the president). Despite the fact that the young chemist had a doctoral degree and some practical experience, his uncle made it clear that his salary would not exceed seven dollars per week.

Armed with some of the award-winning soup recipes he had managed to bring back from Paris, John Dorrance proposed a startling new idea—*condensed* soup. If the water content could be removed from the soup before canning, it would cost less to ship, would take less space on store shelves, and could be sold for less.

This was just the product that Joseph Campbell's company was looking for to meet and beat the competition. So, about the time that the veteran fruit and vegetable man was ready to retire, his company began production of what would soon be its major product.

Joseph Campbell died in 1900 at the age of eighty-three, four years before the Campbell Kids made their appearance in national advertising and immediately captured the hearts of Americans.

Campbell would also have been surprised if he could have foreseen that his familiar red-and-white can of tomato soup would become the subject of a pop art painting that has become a classic. Andy Warhol's realistic rendering of the Campbell's soup can has been displayed in art museums and been reproduced in many art books.

Although he never actually got into the production of soup, Campbell's name will forever be associated with the product. Abraham Anderson's soup company, on the other hand, faded into oblivion.

★ Harland Sanders
(Kentucky Fried Chicken)

Life had never been easy for Harland Sanders. He was born to a poor farm family in Henryville, Indiana, in 1890. His father died when he was only five, leaving the young boy to care for his younger brother and sister while his mother worked.

When he was tall enough to reach the top of the stove, Harland began to cook the family meals. He had no way of knowing at the time, but his mother's cooking lessons would one day lead him to fame and fortune. But first, there would be a lot of rough years to endure.

At age eleven, Harland went to work on a neighboring farm for two dollars a month. He lost the job after only a few weeks because of laziness. He never forgot the tongue-lashing he got from his mother and vowed to work hard the rest of his life.

A year later, Harland's mother married a man who could not get along with the children. Harland, who was already big for his age, suffered the most. One day, his stepfather literally kicked him out of the house. This was the end of his schooling and the beginning of a life of hard work and dead-end jobs.

After working on several farms, Harland moved to New Albany, Indiana, where he got a job collecting fares on streetcars. It wasn't long before he was off to Cuba. An Army recruiter had talked the sixteen-year-old into lying about his age and enlisting.

The homesick private finally returned to the United States and civilian life. He went to work as a blacksmith's helper in a railroad yard and was soon promoted to locomotive fireman. While still in his teens, Harland Sanders got married, and just before the birth of his first child, the feisty young man was fired because of a dispute with his bosses at the railroad.

In the difficult years that followed, Harland Sanders worked as a railroad section hand, insurance agent, steamboat promoter, gaslight manufacturer, justice of the peace, and tire salesman. But as he neared the age of forty, Harland realized that he was tired of working for others and getting nowhere. He wanted a business of his own.

Shortly after the stock market crash of 1929, with the country sinking deeper into the Great Depression, Shell Oil offered Sanders a gas station, rent free, in Corbin, Kentucky. Despite the bad times, Sanders Servistation did well because of the emphasis he placed on the word "service." He washed windshields, filled radiators, and offered free air, even if a motorist just drove in to ask for directions. This kind of customer attention was as rare then as it is today.

Sanders also relied on sales to tourists and business travelers who drove right by his service station on heavily traveled U.S. Highway 25. To augment the meager profits he made from selling gas, Sanders started preparing homemade snacks to serve these hungry travelers.

His first "restaurant" was a small room in the front of the gas station. It had only one table and six chairs. The kitchen was in the living quarters behind the station. When the snack business outgrew the tiny room, the enterprising Sanders opened a larger service station across the road, with room for a real restaurant.

It wasn't long before Sanders Cafe had a reputation for good food. Using his mother's recipes, Sanders cooked up chicken, ham, fresh vegetables, biscuits and honey every day. In 1939, his restaurant was listed in Duncan Hines's respected guidebook, *Adventures in Good Eating*.

Cleanliness became an obsession with Harland Sanders. Weary travelers who were used to dingy roadside diners appreciated the spacious dining room with its homey atmosphere. There were tablecloths and flowers on every table. The floors and restrooms were spotless. Sanders wanted things to be just right for his customers.

The best-selling item on the menu was pan-fried chicken, made with a combination of herbs and spices that Sanders kept perfecting over the years. There was only one problem: preparing fried chicken properly in an iron skillet took half an hour. Travelers in a hurry didn't want to wait that long.

Other restaurants served what was called "southern" fried chicken. Fried in deep fat, it was faster to prepare but was greasy and didn't taste the same.

Then, in the late 1930s, Sanders attended a demonstration of a "newfangled" invention called a pressure cooker. During the demonstration, green beans were cooked in only a few minutes. To Sanders' surprise, they were tasty and perfectly done.

He wondered how chicken would taste when cooked under pressure. He bought one of the pressure cookers and brought it back to his restaurant, where he began experimenting with cooking time, pressure, shortening temperature and amounts. Finally, Harland Sanders came up with the best fried chicken he had ever tasted, done in only eight minutes. He named his creation *Kentucky Fried Chicken.*

Harland Sanders' reputation began to spread far beyond the town of Corbin and the surrounding area. In 1936, Governor Ruby Laffoon bestowed on Sanders the honorary title of Kentucky Colonel. He used the title from then on.

When the restaurant was destroyed by fire in 1939, Sanders rebuilt it and added a motor court that became the first high-quality overnight lodging in southeastern Kentucky. The Colonel greeted every guest personally and made sure that they had a good meal to go with their comfortable room. A note across the bottom of the menu read, "Not worth the price, but mighty good."

Then, in the mid-1950s, disaster struck in an unexpected way. Plans were announced that a new superhighway, Interstate 75, would be built seven miles west of U.S. 25. This meant that Sanders Court and Cafe would be completely isolated from the automobile traffic that had passed right by its front door.

Sanders was forced to put his businesses up for sale. A few years earlier he had turned down an offer of $164,000 for the motel, cafe, and service station. Now, at auction, they sold for only $75,000. He paid off his outstanding debts and found himself, once again, nearly broke with a monthly Social Security check of $105 as his only income.

Although he was sixty-six years old, the Colonel felt he was too young to retire. The franchise business was just beginning to take off in the mid-sixties, and the tireless inventor of Kentucky Fried Chicken wondered if his unique cooking process would sell in other parts of the country.

Loading up his 1946 Ford with his trusty pressure cooker and a fifty-pound can of his famous seasoning (the secret recipe of eleven herbs and spices was locked up in his head), Colonel Sanders set out for Indiana and Ohio.

He visited one restaurant after another, offering to cook chicken for the owner and his employees. If they liked the way it tasted, he offered to sell them his secret seasoning (but not the secret) and teach them how to cook the chicken, and they would pay him four cents for each dinner sold. Each deal was closed with a handshake, and the sales reports were handled on the honor system.

Sanders hoped to generate an income of, maybe, $12,000 a year. By 1960 he had sold 190 franchises. Three years later, there were 600 in the United States and Canada and the Colonel was depositing $1,000 a day in the bank.

It was during this time that Sanders began to dress like a Kentucky Colonel. But it happened by accident. While in Colorado, he was asked to appear on a television talk show. The only clean suit he had was a white Palm Beach. Viewers reacted positively to the sight of the distinguished man with the white hair, white goatee, and white suit. From then on, he was never seen in public without the distinctive outfit. He wore out eight white suits a year.

In 1964, a twenty-nine-year-old Louisville lawyer named John Y. Brown, Jr., (who would later become governor of Kentucky), and a sixty-year-old Nashville businessman named Jack Massey offered to buy the Colonel's business for $2 million and the guarantee of a lifetime job. The Colonel accepted. Seven years later, Kentucky

Fried Chicken was sold to Heublein, Inc., for $275 million.

Instead of sitting back in a rocking chair and counting his money, the Colonel traveled all over the country as a goodwill ambassador. When asked why he kept working so hard, he'd reply, "Work never hurt anyone. More people rust out than wear out."

When death finally came at the age of ninety, the body of the beloved Colonel lay in state in the rotunda of the state capitol in Frankfort, Kentucky, with the towering statue of Abraham Lincoln looking down on the open casket. It was a fitting tribute. Both were rugged individualists who had survived hardships to make something of their lives.

★ Dwight Hamilton Baldwin
(Baldwin Pianos)

1862 was not the best year to start a new business. The Civil War was raging and the nation's economy was on shaky ground. Nevertheless, forty-one-year-old Dwight Baldwin decided to open a retail piano store in Cincinnati, Ohio.

The Pennsylvania native had always dreamed of becoming a minister. His parents were both active leaders in the Presbyterian church. At nineteen, Baldwin entered Oberlin College to study for the ministry, but because of his frail health he was advised to abandon his studies. In those days, circuit riding parsons had to be robust to endure the rigors of traveling long distances on horse-back from one remote town to another.

The young man's second love was music. He had been a student of the violin since childhood. Leaving Oberlin College, Baldwin began teaching vocal music in several small towns in Ohio and Kentucky, accompanying his pupils on the violin. In 1856, he moved to Cincinnati, where he was offered a job teaching music in the public schools. His salary was one hundred dollars a month, or twelve hundred dollars a year. (Regular school teachers made six hundred dollars or less a year.)

In the seven years he spent in Cincinnati, Dwight Baldwin taught over one hundred thousand students. He must have made quite an impression on those young people, for many would return to seek his advice about buying a piano or reed organ. They obviously had confidence in his honesty and musical judgment. As the requests for advice increased, the music teacher began to think seriously of becoming an agent for the sale of musical instruments.

Through the years, Baldwin lived frugally and managed to save two thousand dollars. In 1862, he left the teaching profession and used his life savings to buy several pianos and reed organs to stock his first retail store.

His desire was to sell the best musical instruments on the market. He chose Chickering pianos because he believed they were inexpensive, durable, and had a superior tone. Later, he became a dealer for the prestigious Steinway pianos.

Although successful, Dwight Baldwin recognized that business was not one of his strong points. He did have a talent, however, for hiring promising individuals with exceptional minds for business matters.

One of those bright young men was Lucien Wulsin, who was originally hired as bookkeeper. Wulsin, who was twenty-four years younger than Baldwin, was soon made a partner and became the active business head of the firm.

In 1887, Steinway and Sons suddenly and without warning dropped Baldwin as a dealer of their pianos and gave the franchise to a Boston firm that had just opened a store in Cincinnati. To add insult to injury, the new competitor promptly hired several of Baldwin's employees.

After the devastating loss, it was Lucien Wulsin who convinced his partner to start manufacturing his own pianos. The Baldwin name was already respected in the music community. A piano with that name on it, Wulsin was convinced, would have a ready-made market.

It took over a year to design "the best piano that could be built." In the meantime, Baldwin established the Hamilton Organ Company in Illinois and manufacturing operations were set up in rented facilities in Chicago. A year later, the Baldwin Piano Company was incorporated in Cincinnati.

For more than a century and a quarter, the Baldwin Piano and Organ Company has done more than provide quality instruments. Through its artistic program and support of musical education, the company has been one of this country's greatest promoters of music. Their retail finance programs have enabled hundreds of enterprising individuals to open their own retail music businesses to serve their communities.

Baldwin ultimately succeeded because of a business loss that led to a new-found opportunity. Necessity truly is the mother of invention.

★ Richard Samuel Reynolds
(Reynolds Aluminum)

Richard Reynolds, born in 1881, was only thirteen when he entered Kings College, after attending public schools in his native Bristol, Tennessee. At a time when most teenagers were finishing high school, young Richard graduated from college and went on to Columbia University and the University of Virginia.

While Richard was studying at the University of Virginia, his uncle—tobacco king R. J. Reynolds—persuaded him to leave school and come to work for him in Winston-Salem, North Carolina.

The young man more than earned his pay of fifty dollars a month. He persuaded his uncle to switch from chewing tobacco to smoking tobacco. His idea of blending mild Kentucky burley and the stronger Virginia tobacco led to the introduction of Camel cigarettes, which was to become one of the nation's best-sellers. Richard also invented the tobacco tin for Prince Albert pipe tobacco, which locked in moisture.

In those early days, cigarettes and loose tobacco were wrapped in thin sheets of tin and lead. The technology of tinfoil production fascinated Richard Reynolds. As World War I came to an end, Reynolds left his uncle's employ to start the U. S. Foil Company in Louisville, Kentucky.

Reynolds supplied tin-lead wraps to the tobacco industry as well as makers of hard candy who found that foil gave a tighter seal against moisture than wax paper. Then, in the mid-1920s, aluminum became popular.

Aluminum is the most abundant metal on earth and is incredibly versatile. It is lightweight yet strong, tough yet pliable. It conducts electricity, yet reflects heat. It resists corrosion, yet can be recycled—which has become so important today.

As the price of aluminum came down in 1928, the Reynolds Metals Company was formed and the first aluminum foil plant was built in Louisville. Richard Reynolds believed that this lightweight and nonrusting material would have a bright future.

When the Aluminum Corporation of America (Alcoa) could not supply him with all the raw material he needed, Reynolds decided to go into the production of aluminum himself. Today, Reynolds is the second largest aluminum producer in the United States.

The symbol of the Reynolds Metals Company is Saint George holding a shield and sword as he battles a dragon. The warrior on horseback could easily represent the founder, Richard Reynolds, who successfully challenged the giant (Alcoa) and became an innovator, pioneer, and a leader in the aluminum industry.

★ Jerome Smucker
(Smucker's Jams and Jellies)

"With a name like Smucker's, it has to be good." That's how television commercials have been promoting a line of jams and jellies that have captured the hearts and taste buds of Americans for generations.

No one had to invent the unusual brand name. There really was a Jerome Smucker. He lived in Orville, Ohio, and made a modest living making and selling apple cider during the latter part of the nineteenth century.

When the apple cider season was over each year, Smucker's mill stood idle. One day he found an old family recipe for apple butter and decided to put it to good use. Local farmers were invited to bring their surplus apples to his mill and Smucker would turn the surplus fruit into apple butter.

Word traveled fast and it wasn't long before city dwellers were asking to buy the popular spread. Smucker had to expand his mill in order to supply grocery stores with gallon and half-gallon crocks of his apple butter.

In 1923, Smucker added jams and jellies to his line. Although the J. M. Smucker Company still makes apple butter, their best-selling products today are strawberry preserves and grape jelly.

★ Earl V. Wise
(Wise Potato Chips)

Eleven years before Herman Lay began selling potato chips from the back of his Model A Ford (see Chapter 1), a man named Earl V. Wise was operating a grocery store in Berwick, Pennsylvania. In the spring of 1921 he found himself with an oversupply of potatoes. Potato chips were becoming a popular snack food, so Wise sliced and cooked his surplus spuds and put them on sale in the store. His customers liked the chips so much that Wise had to buy more potatoes to meet the demand.

The tasty chips were soon being sold in other stores, but since they were packaged in ordinary brown paper bags, no one knew who had made them. Earl Wise knew he had to find a more attractive and identifying package.

In the early 1930s he pioneered the use of cellophane bags. An advertising agency created the symbol of Peppy the Owl to decorate the new packages. The Wise old owl attracted shoppers' attention for decades. Today the owl's eye is used to dot the "i" in Wise.

★ 8 ★

Accidents
Will Happen

An accident has been described as "a surprise arranged by nature." An astute observer of human behavior has suggested that "absence of mind causes most accidents, but presence of mind can turn an accident into a discovery or a business opportunity."

That is exactly what happened to six individuals who left their mark—and their brand—on the American business scene.

★ Charles Goodyear
(Goodyear Tire & Rubber Co.)

Charles Goodyear was born in 1800 in New Haven, Connecticut, the son of a small manufacturer. Enjoying a normal childhood in this small community, the young boy never dreamed that one day there would be blimps hovering over the country bearing his name.

Charles had shown an interest in studying for the ministry, but family finances kept him from going beyond high school. Besides, his practical father thought Charles would make a good merchant in the family's new hardware business.

When the depression of 1820 hit the nation, the firm of A. Goodyear & Sons went under, along with hundreds of other small businesses. Charles, barely out of his teens, assumed responsibility for his elderly father's debts and made the first of what would be many trips to debtors' prison.

Early in the 1830s, Goodyear traveled to New York City in an attempt to raise another loan. While walking along a Manhattan street, he noticed a number of rubber goods in a store window.

Rubber had been introduced to the Western world when Christopher Columbus came back from Santo Domingo with a few of the bouncing balls that the natives had played games with. No practical application was found for the mysterious gum elastic until late in the eighteenth century, when someone noticed that it could rub out pencil marks. This discovery gave the substance

its name, *rubber*, and a small market was created
for this South American curiosity.

By the time Goodyear became interested in
the product, a rubber mania had swept the country, but it ended as quickly as it had started. The
buying public soon became fed up with the messy
stuff that turned soft and sticky in the heat of
summer and hard and brittle in winter. Not one
of the rubber companies that had sprung up during the craze survived. Millions of dollars were
lost. Everyone agreed that rubber was over and
done with in America.

But Charles Goodyear was fascinated with
the product and soon became obsessed by the
challenge of refining rubber into something usa-
ble and useful. "There is probably no other inert
substance which so excites the mind," he was to
say at a later date.

Goodyear returned home from New York
and was once again put in prison for nonpay-
ment of bills. Jail was becoming a familiar place
for him. Not wanting to lose any time, he asked
his wife to bring him a batch of raw rubber and
a rolling pin. In his debtor's cell, he began his
first rubber experiments, kneading and working
the gum for hours at a time.

If rubber is naturally adhesive, he reasoned,
why couldn't a dry powder be mixed in to absorb
the stickiness? He tried magnesia powder with
some encouraging results. But when he and his
family made several hundred pairs of rubber
overshoes using the new magnesia formula, he
watched them all sag into a shapeless, sticky mess.

With each disappointment, he renewed his

efforts with a determination that bordered on fanaticism. After five futile years of failed attempts and some near-misses, Charles Goodyear had hit bottom. Farmers around Woburn, Massachusetts, where he now lived, gave his children milk and let them dig up half-grown potatoes for food.

The great discovery came in the winter of 1839. Goodyear was using sulphur in his experiments now. One day, according to the most reliable story, he walked into the general store to show off his latest formula. Some of the old men who always hung around the store looked up and snickered when the hapless inventor walked in. Some may even have made some remarks about the shabby way he was treating his wife and children.

The usually mild-mannered little man got so angry that he waved the sample of rubber-and-sulphur he was carrying. It flew from his fingers and landed on top of the sizzling-hot potbelly stove.

When he went to scrape it off, he was astonished to find that the gum had not melted, but had charred into something that looked like leather. It was so dramatically changed that he knew he had finally created weatherproof rubber.

This discovery has often been cited as one of history's most celebrated accidents, but Goodyear strongly denied it. The hot stove incident, he said later, held meaning only for the man "whose mind was prepared to draw an inference."

All was not over for Goodyear. He knew that heat and sulphur were the magic ingredients that changed rubber. But how much heat, and for how long? The experiments were to continue for some time before he finally hit on the right formula. He pawned his watch and the household furniture, and when even the dinnerware was gone, he made rubber dishes to eat from!

A trip to Boston to seek more financial backing ended in another jail sentence when he couldn't pay his five-dollar hotel bill. When he returned home, he found that his infant son had died. (Of the twelve Goodyear children, six died in infancy.)

Was Goodyear the victim of circumstance or was he his own worst enemy? When he finally began to realize an income from his important discovery, he sold the manufacturing rights that might have made him a millionaire. The licensing deals for the dozens of patents he held were so poorly written that Goodyear received very little money for all his efforts. When he died in 1860, he left two-hundred-thousand dollars in unpaid debts.

As for the billion-dollar Goodyear Tire & Rubber Company—the world's largest rubber enterprise—it was named in his honor, but neither Charles nor his family were ever connected with it.

★ Thomas Adams, Sr.
(Adams Chewing Gum)

Thomas Adams was born in New York City in 1818 and orphaned at the age of nine. As so often happens to highly intelligent, inventive individuals with many talents, young Thomas could not seem to find a job worthy of his genius.

Photography, which was then in its infancy, interested him. He became a daguerrotypist and was evidently good enough to be appointed a military photographer when he enlisted at the outbreak of the Civil War. But his inventive streak needed some outlet.

After the war, he devised a burner for kerosene lamps and a horse feed bag that enjoyed wide use, but most of his gadgets brought little or no remuneration. He finally realized he had to do something practical, so he went into the wholesale glass business and opened a store in lower Manhattan, just a block from where the Staten Island ferry docked. With that move, he became the right man in the right place at the right time.

Destiny had already put into place the second character who would play a key role in this drama of chance and coincidence. That person was Antonio Lopez de Santa Anna, who had led a force of over six thousand men across the Rio Grande to storm and destroy the Alamo in San Antonio, Texas. After a siege that lasted several days, Santa Anna's men massacred the survivors, including Davy Crockett and Jim Bowie.

The Mexican general served several terms as president of Mexico, before and after the Alamo incident, then left his country and lived for five years on Staten Island in New York City.

The catalyst who brought the Mexican *caudillo* and the Yankee inventor together was Rudolph Napegy, Santa Anna's personal secretary, who often took the ferry from Staten Island to Manhattan to shop and run errands for his employer. Napegy must have visited Adams's shop several times, and the two developed an acquaintanceship, during which Napegy learned of Adams's inventive talents. Napegy reported his "find" to Santa Anna, who seemed very pleased.

Like most deposed dictators before and since, Santa Anna needed money to raise an army in order to march on and "liberate" his country. When he left Mexico, he took with him a rather large amount of chicle, a gummy substance from the sapodilla trees that grow in Mexico. For years, efforts had been made to turn the dried sap into a substitute for rubber, but no one had been able to succeed. Santa Anna believed that a good Yankee inventor could do the job. His secretary, Rudolph Napegy, convinced him that Thomas Adams was the man.

The meeting took place in Santa Anna's stone house in Sailor's Snug Harbor on Staten Island.

"I need millions, Señor Adams," Santa Anna said through his secretary-interpreter. "Here is the treasure of Mexico," he continued as Napegy brought in and opened the bag of chicle. "This is the latex of the sapodilla tree which we have in great abundance in my country, and you can convert it into a rubber substitute!" He told Adams that Mexicans had chewed chicle since the time of the Aztecs, but that no one had fully realized the true potential of the sticky stuff. It would be like manna from heaven for both of them.

The convincing exiled general arranged with friends in Mexico to send Adams a ton of chicle, which Adams paid for. With the help of his four sons, the inventor set about the impossible task of turning the gummy resin into a new kind of rubber. The Adams men (father and sons) worked in the family kitchen in New Jersey, boiling and refining the chicle. But no matter how hard they tried, the mass lacked elasticity, resiliency, and durability. Adams was ready to quit, but fate intervened once more.

Adams had just about made up his mind to throw all of the chicle away, when he happened into a drugstore one day just as a little girl came in and asked for a penny's worth of chewing gum. When the girl left, Adams asked the proprietor what the chewing gum was made of and learned that it was paraffin, which, the druggist told him, made poor chewing gum.

In that instant, Adams knew that he had found the right use for the chicle that had filled up his house and his life for about a year. Adams and his four sons went to work immediately. They took some of the chicle and let it soak in hot water until it was the consistency of putty. It was no longer brownish black, but a grayish white color. Chewing gum had been created.

The men kneaded it and rolled the substance into little balls—two hundred of them! Adams delivered the unsweetened gum balls to the Jersey City drugstore owner, who promised to display them on the counter. Adams was evidently not too hopeful for immediate success, for he warned the druggist that the supply might last as long as three months. To his surprise and delight, the two hundred gum balls sold out before noon that day.

The encouraging news spurred the Adams family into action. They pooled their meager resources—somewhere between thirty-five dollars and fifty-five dollars—and went into business.

The oldest son, Thomas Adams, Jr., was a salesman who traveled as far west as the Mississippi. He agreed to take a supply of the gum on his next trip and try to sell it along the way. But there was something missing—a brand name. After some deliberation, it was decided to call it *Adams' New York Gum No. 1—Snapping and Stretching*.

The chewing gum proved to be an instant success as orders began to pour in. The fledgling chewing gum industry got stuck in controversy, however, when puritanical reformers were convinced that gum was a vice, and some would-be "scientists" spread the word that chewing gum was really made of horses' hooves and glue. The public's need for a "good chew" won out, and the Adams name became widely known.

With his business on a solid footing, Thomas Adams's next project was to put some flavoring in the tasteless chicle. His first attempt, sassafras, was scrapped. Then he turned to a licorice-anise flavor, and *Adams' Black Jack Gum* was the result. It is still made by the American Chicle Company and is the oldest flavored chewing gum on the market today.

★ Edward and Clarence Scott
(Scott Paper Products)

Edward and Clarence were born in Saratoga County, New York, but had moved to Philadelphia by the time they began a paper business. One of the products they decided to make was toilet paper, and their timing could not have been better.

The first commercially packaged toilet tissue in America was introduced in 1857 by a businessman named Joseph Gayetty. But the product, which was sold in packages of individual sheets, sold poorly because Americans could not see spending good money on clean new paper when bathrooms and outhouses were stacked with perfectly good old newspapers and outdated catalogs.

In England, a manufacturer named Walter Alcock came out with toilet tissue on a roll that was perforated into squares. He had a good idea, but his problem was how to advertise it in the prudish atmosphere of the Victorian era.

As homes, hotels, and restaurants in the United States began to be built with indoor plumbing systems, people became more receptive to toilet paper. Scotts' tissues were packaged in small rolls and sold in plain brown wrappers. When a newly designed toilet bowl—the one-piece ceramic "Pedestal Vase"—won a gold medal in design, the Scott brothers thought it was time to replace the unlabeled brown wrapper with a more decorative label, and the prestigious name

"Waldorf Tissues" was given to it. Today, it is known simply as *ScotTissue*.

So much for toilet paper. It was a factory error that resulted in the creation of a brand-new product.

By 1907, the Scott brothers' paper company was a business success. Their high-quality, soft bathroom tissue was a favorite of consumers. The tissues were manufactured at a large paper mill and shipped to the Scott plant in long units called "parent rolls." These were then cut down to bathroom-size packages. One day, an order from the mill was discovered to be defective. The paper was unusually heavy and wrinkled, unfit for the Scott name.

The shipment was scheduled to be returned, when a member of the Scott family suggested perforating the thick paper into small towel-size sheets. Because of an accident in manufacture, the first disposable paper towels were "invented."

The towels debuted in 1907 under the name "Sani-Towel" and were sold primarily to hotels, restaurants, and railroad stations for use in public washrooms. Selling the general public was a different matter. Just as they had objected to buying toilet tissues years before, they now griped about paying good money for towels that would be used just once and then thrown away, when cloth towels are washed and used over and over again.

In 1931, the towels were renamed *ScotTowels* and a roll of two-hundred sheets sold for a quarter. As home owners discovered more uses for disposable towels, the sales went up—as did the fortunes of Edward and Clarence Scott.

★ William Procter and James Gamble
(Procter & Gamble)

William Procter and James Gamble had a lot in common. They had both come to the United States from the British Isles—William from England and James from Northern Ireland. They both ended up in Cincinnati and, within months of each other, married sisters.

They didn't know it at the time, but the two brothers-in-law were to be linked in the minds of the buying public long after they were gone. Even today, who can think of Procter without Gamble?

But at the beginning, they were really competitors. Procter was a candlemaker and Gamble, a soapmaker. They competed for the same supply of animal fats to make their respective products. Their father-in-law, Alexander Norris, thought this didn't make sense. He finally convinced them to become partners.

In the early part of 1837, the two men joined forces. James Gamble supervised production and William Procter was in charge of the office and sales. Candles were their principal source of income, but it was soap that would earn them fame and fortune.

There were eighteen soap and candle manufacturers in Cincinnati at the time. The ethical standards of the P & G partners contrasted sharply with the unscrupulous practices of the others. Many used fraudulent claims in their advertising. The superior product turned out by Procter and Gamble spoke for itself, and their business enjoyed a steady growth.

Most of the soap manufactured in the United States in those days was for laundry or household use. Gentle castile soap had to be imported, and it was expensive. By the time the second generation was ready to take over the business, the Procter and Gamble company was still searching for a white soap equal in quality to castile but not as expensive.

James Gamble, the cofounder's son, finally succeeded. The milky white soap he created was effective enough to be used as a laundry soap, yet mild enough for a baby's bath. It was to be called *P & G White Soap*, but Harley Procter, son of William Procter and cousin of the soap's creator, James, thought the name was as colorless as the product itself.

One Sunday, while at church, Harley's mind was jolted back to reality when he heard the pastor begin reading from Psalm 45:8 and these words grabbed his attention: "All thy garments smell of myrrh and aloes and cassia, out of the ivory palaces whereby they have made thee glad."

Ivory. *Ivory!* That was the word he was looking for. Ivory was white and it reminded him of purity. P & G's White Soap now had a distinctive name that would serve it well. But it was actually a manufacturing accident that created the Ivory soap we have today.

To understand the blunder, one must understand the process of soapmaking at the time. The ingredients were mixed in huge vats by mechanical blades. The metal arms revolved in the mixture until an attendant decided by sight and smell that the batch was thick enough to be poured into soap frames. There it would cool and harden into cakes of soap before being wrapped.

One day, the attendant went off to lunch and forgot to turn the machine off. When he returned about an hour later, he found that the frothy mixture had overflowed the vat. Not wanting to waste an entire batch, his supervisor decided to pour the mixture into the frames. The ingredients had not changed, he reasoned. So what if there was a little too much air in the foamy mixture?

The incident was forgotten until orders began pouring in from all over the country, asking for more of "that soap that floats." When Harley and James investigated, they learned about the frothy batch. A decision was made to duplicate the mistake and advertise the soap's new and unique advantage: "It floats!"

But novelty was not what Procter and Gamble was all about. Harley Procter was so determined to maintain the high standards set by his father and uncle that he hired an independent scientific laboratory to verify the purity of Ivory Soap. The results revealed that the impurities amounted to only 0.56 percent. Turning the negative information into a positive statement, Harley Procter coined the most famous advertising slogan of all time: "Ivory Soap is 99 and 44/100 percent pure."

★ 9 ★

Failure Is Not
the End

Bankruptcy is not the dreaded word it used to be. Every year, approximately half a million people and businesses file for voluntary bankruptcy as a legal way to get out of paying their debts. A cynic would define bankruptcy as putting your money in your pants and giving your coat to your creditor.

In the early part of this century, however, bankruptcy was a shame to be avoided under all circumstances, and the victim would do anything to pay back every penny he or she owed. In this chapter you will meet four individuals who experienced business failure and bankruptcy in the early part of their careers, even several times, and were able to bounce back because they believed in themselves.

★ James A. Folger
(Folger's Coffee)

Exactly two hundred years before James Folger was born on Nantucket Island, off the coast of Massachusetts, the first Folger arrived on these shores from Norwich, England. Peter Folger and his wife, Mary, had eight children. The youngest child, a girl named Abiah, grew up to become the mother of Benjamin Franklin.

James Folger was one of nine children born to a blacksmith who had become prosperous when he began repairing the big whaling vessels that sailed from the harbor. He soon had enough money to buy two ships of his own.

Several tragedies befell the Folger family during James's early years. His father's business faced hard times when the whaling business went into a decline. Then his nineteen-year-old brother died and, two years later, a fire broke out in the business section of Nantucket that completely destroyed thirty-three acres of land and his father's two ships.

When news of the discovery of vast gold deposits in California reached the East Coast, the Folger boys were anxious to try their luck. In the late fall of 1849, they waved good-bye to their parents and boarded a ship for the long journey.

They did not arrive in San Francisco until May of the following year.

In only two years, San Francisco had grown from eight hundred to forty thousand inhabitants, most of them bearded males between the ages of twenty and forty. The bawdy town had become nothing more than a starting point for the actual mining operations about one hundred miles away.

Shortly after the brothers' arrival in San Franciso, James Folger landed a sales job for a spice and coffee mill. The mill was owned by two men, William Bovee and Ira Marden. Bovee, who, like the Folgers, had come to California in search of gold, built the mill with the confidence that there would be a ready market for coffee that was already roasted, ground, and packaged in convenient bags. It was an idea that had never been tried before.

As a salesman, James traveled up and down the hills of California, selling his wares to eager customers. After a year, he thought it was time he tried his luck at prospecting. William Bovee also decided to return to the Sierras in search of gold, and he sold part of the coffee and spice business.

James Folger was one of the fortunate ones— he made a strike. He used the money to open a supply store in the middle of the mining region, and two years later he returned to San Francisco with a handsome profit.

Bovee returned to San Francisco and sold all but a small portion of the business to James Folger. The mill was renamed Marden & Folger. When an economic slump hit after the Civil War, the partners couldn't pay the company's debts and were forced into bankruptcy.

Folger went to his creditors and explained the situation, persuading them to let him continue running the business. The creditors believed in James Folger and gave him another chance. He was soon back in business, roasting, grinding, and selling his coffee. This time, his name alone was on the bags. He had bought out his partner with a promissory note for his share of the business. Although it took him almost ten years, all the creditors and his former partner were paid in full.

★ Rowland Hussy Macy
(Macy's Department Stores)

After a four-year stint aboard a whaling ship, Macy had tried several jobs in Boston before he opened his first store, a needle-and-thread business. It lasted only a few months. The next year, Macy tried again with a small dry-goods store. After two years, he made a final entry in his account book: "I have worked two years for nothing."

In 1849, Macy and one of his brothers joined the California gold rush and opened a general store near San Francisco. Even this venture did not fare well, and he soon returned to New England.

The stubborn and quick-tempered Macy refused to accept defeat. He opened his fourth store in Haverhill, Massachusetts. It was here that he began to show his merchandising talents.

He called his store "The Haverhill Cheap Store," and it lived up to its name. Macy participated in price wars with its competitors and ran newspaper advertisements every day. The stock was expanded to include "notions and fancy goods."

It was during this period that Macy decided on two business principles that were to make his store unique. All sales were on a cash basis. He did not extend credit even to his own family. He also instituted fixed prices on all merchandise. There was no more need to haggle over prices, because they were already set as low as they could be.

Despite these sound business practices, the Haverhill Cheap Store went bankrupt four years after it opened. Macy knew he had found a successful formula, but he needed a bigger city in which to operate. New York City seemed to be the place.

At the age of thirty-six, with four strikes against him, Rowland Macy opened for business on Fourteenth Street and Sixth Avenue. With intensive advertising, the small dry-goods store quickly expanded to a department store—a term that had not yet been coined. The dauntless merchant was finally on his way.

Today, Macy's is the world's biggest store, and it never would have happened if Rowland Macy had not believed that "failure is not the end."

★ Henry Ford
(Ford Automobiles)

The country was in the middle of the Civil War when Henry Ford was born on a Michigan farm in 1863. Like many American boys of the last century, Henry had to help work the land, but he found farming dull, except for tinkering with the farm equipment. He had a gift for looking at a machine and quickly understanding how it worked, how to repair it, and how to make it work better.

Two eventful things happened during Henry's twelfth year. On one of the rural roads, he saw his first horseless carriage. The wagon was propelled by steam from a coal boiler on board. Henry was so impressed that four years later he built one for himself just to test his mechanical skills.

Also at twelve, he was given his first watch. He finally had a mechanical device that he could take apart and put together whenever he wanted to. There is no telling how often that watch was dismantled, but by the time Henry Ford left school, he had become an expert watchmaker. His goal was to make a watch so cheaply that it could be sold for only a dollar.

At age seventeen, with his brief formal education behind him and against his father's wishes, Ford walked the nine miles from the farm to the city of Detroit, which had already become the mechanics capital of the country. He found a job as a repairman in a machine shop, and on the side he repaired watches for friends and fellow employees.

Ford's dream of manufacturing a popular-priced watch faded when he read an article in an English magazine, giving a complete technical description of the new internal combustion machine. With this gasoline-powered engine, Ford knew, a new industry was about to be born and he wanted to be a part of it.

Henry Ford did not invent the automobile. That honor goes to Gottlieb Daimler, who demonstrated his first gasoline-powered motorcar in Paris in 1887. Charles Duryea came out with the first gasoline-powered motorcar in the United States in 1892. These early models were made entirely by hand and were not only very expensive but very unreliable. The cars often broke down and had to be repaired. Ford wanted to change all that.

In 1899, a group of businessmen invested fifteen thousand dollars to help Henry Ford start the Detroit Automobile Company. The few cars that were made were too expensive for the goal that Henry had set. His investors did not share his views about making cars for the masses. The arguments continued until the following year, when the Detroit Automobile Company went bankrupt.

Recovering from his defeat, Ford decided that the way to call attention to himself and get ahead of the competition was to go into racing. He won his first auto race and became a celebrity overnight. Two years later, at the age of forty, he set out to form the Ford Motor Company. Twelve investors put up a total of twenty-eight thousand dollars in working capital.

The first car was called the Model A and could travel at a speed of twenty miles per hour. In a period of fifteen months, seventeen hundred cars were sold, and a few are still running today. Although it was a dependable car, Henry Ford was not satisfied. He knew he could do better. During the next five years, Ford and his engineers came out with one model after another, going through the alphabet from B to S. Some of the models were completely unsatisfactory and were never offered for sale.

In 1908, Ford came out with the Model T and the search for the right car was over. It was a brilliantly simple machine. If anything went wrong, most owners would be able to fix it. The Model T caught on immediately with the public. The $850 price tag was a definite advantage, and over the next nineteen years, the price kept coming down until it reached $265.

As demand for the car increased, the need to speed up production became painfully obvious. Ford did not invent the production-line concept, but he adapted it to the automobile industry. He developed a moving belt that was strong enough to carry cars along an assembly line from one worker to the next. The time it took to assemble an automobile was reduced from twelve hours and twenty-eight minutes to only ninety-eight minutes, thereby vastly increasing the rate at which cars were produced. Seven years later, Ford realized his "life's desire"—to turn out a car every minute.

In the nearly two decades of production, over fifteen million Model T Fords were produced and sold. They were finally discontinued in 1927 when consumers demanded a change, including more elegant styling and solid comfort. Henry Ford obliged by going back to the head of the alphabet and coming out with a new, improved Model A.

What astonished Ford's competitors the most about the Model T was that the color never changed through all those years. The uniformity, of course, was one reason why Ford could turn out so many cars in such a short time. "Let them have any color they want," Ford once said, "so long as it's black."

The Ford Motor Company also stayed in the black. After a shaky start, including the bankruptcy of his first company, Henry Ford became one of the wealthiest industrialists of his time.

Every year on his birthday, Ford put on one old shoe to remind himself that he had once been poor and might be poor again. But he didn't hoard his money. In 1936, most of his wealth went to establish the Ford Foundation, which has supported programs in developing countries around the world and helped advance opportunities for low-income groups here at home.

In 1955, the Ford Foundation granted the largest single philanthropic gift ever made—five hundred million dollars—to over four thousand privately supported colleges, universities, medical schools, and hospitals.

It was the common people who bought the

affordable cars that Ford turned out by the millions, and he wanted to return to the world a portion of what he had received. Henry Ford knew that it is only what we give away that lasts.

★ Henry John Heinz
   (H. J. Heinz Co.)

Henry Heinz was the oldest of nine children born to German immigrants in Sharpsburg, Pennsylvania. Almost every family in town had a garden, but the Heinz vegetable garden was so big and the produce of such superior quality that neighbors began to ask if they could purchase some of the surplus.

At the age of eight, Henry began to peddle the produce to other families in town, carrying a basket in each hand. He did so well that by the time he was ten, he had to use a wheelbarrow.

To encourage the boy and give him some practical business training, young Henry was given three-quarters of an acre of land to work with. At twelve, he enlarged his garden to over three acres, bought a horse and cart, and included local merchants among his customers.

The experience he gained during those early years would stay with him for the rest of his life. The name of H. J. Heinz would forever be associated with food and food processing.

In his twenty-fifth year, Henry Heinz married the daughter of an Irish immigrant and, together with a partner, founded a company to grow and bottle food. Heinz and Noble started their business selling horseradish, which until then was imported from Europe. They grew the pungent plant on a small piece of land they had purchased, and bottled it in the old homestead which his father had built and recently vacated.

Producing a homemade product of superior quality caused the rapid growth of Heinz, Noble and Company. Within five years, the firm had added sauerkraut, pickles, and vinegar to their line of products.

In 1873, a major financial crisis hit the United States. The New York Stock Exchange closed its doors for ten days, businesses began to fail, and massive unemployment spread throughout the nation. By the beginning of 1875, the effects had reached Sharpsburg. Heinz and his partner had overextended themselves in trying to finance their growing business, and no new bank loans were available.

It was soon evident that Heinz, Noble and Company was in trouble. The county sheriff placed a levy on Henry's household goods, his father's house and furniture, and the company's food stock, horses, and equipment. Henry was arrested twice and twice released on bail. The headlines in the Pittsburgh newspaper announced that the company was "in a pickle."

Crushed but not beaten, Henry Heinz started over again the next year, this time under his own name—H. J. Heinz Company. In his pocket he carried a small notebook marked "M.O.," which stood for "moral obligations." It included a list of all the people to whom he owed money. Although he had no legal obligation to do so, Heinz made sure that each creditor was paid back every penny from the profits of his new company.

★ 10 ★

Religion
and Business

Can business and religion mix? Is it possible to operate a company on moral principles and still make a profit?

Henry J. Heinz (see Chapter 9) grew up in a strict Lutheran home. Although he was brilliant when it came to promoting his company and its products, he never allowed his advertisements to run in Sunday newspapers.

The following entrepreneurs are just a few of the many successful business people who were able to mix faith and finance, ethics and economics. They all would have agreed with the motto: "Honesty is the one business policy that will never have to be changed to keep up with the times."

★ William Colgate
(Colgate Toothpaste)

Twelve-year-old William Colgate came to the United States during George Washington's second term as president. William's father, Robert, was a political refugee who had sided with the colonists in their fight for freedom and independence from England.

William grew up on a farm in Delaware County, New York, but left for New York City as soon as he turned twenty-one. For two years he worked as a laborer for a tallow chandler, making candles and soap from animal fats. In 1806, Colgate opened his own factory and shop on the southern tip of Manhattan.

By 1850, W. B. Colgate and Company was making a hundred different kinds of soap, from the hardest laundry soap to the fanciest perfumed soap. During the years of his firm's steady growth, William Colgate gave one-tenth of all his income to church and charitable activities. For the last eight years of his life, he was treasurer of the America Bible Society, which he helped to organize. William Colgate died in 1857.

Believing that money was meant to be put to good use, Colgate helped start a theological seminary in Hamilton, New York. By the time it became Madison University, the Colgate family had contributed nearly three-quarters of the entire funding. In 1890, the name of the school was changed again, to Colgate University.

★ John Harvard
(Harvard University)

John Harvard was born in London, England, in 1607. His father, a butcher and tavern owner who had been married twice, died of the plague when John was eighteen.

After receiving both a bachelor of arts and a master of arts degree from Cambridge, Harvard sailed for New England with his new bride and settled in Charlestown, now part of Boston. Although he was never formally ordained, Harvard served as a minister for a short time.

When he died, he left his library of 400 books and half of his fortune (it amounted to no more than 375 pounds) to the little college in Newtowne that had been founded just two years before. At the time, it consisted of only a farmhouse surrounded by a one-acre cow pasture.

The Massachusetts General Court named the school in his honor. Harvard University is now the oldest institution of higher learning in the United States.

★ Will Keith Kellogg
(Kellogg's Cereals)

Dr. John Kellogg was superintendent of the Adventist Sanitarium in Battle Creek, Michigan. His younger brother, Will, spent twenty-five years at the "San" as bookkeeper, cashier, packing and shipping clerk, errand boy, and general flunky for his domineering brother.

The two brothers spent many hours creating substitutes for the foods that Seventh-Day Adventists were not allowed to eat—tea, coffee, spices, and meat. The vegetarian diets at the sanitarium were healthy but tasteless. Dr. John invented granola, peanut butter, and a coffee substitute made from cereal.

In 1894, Dr. John and Will were looking for a digestible substitute for bread and came up with a precooked flaked cereal. The toasted flakes of wheat became an instant favorite with the patients. Later, corn flakes were added to the menu.

When patients left the facility, they asked if they could buy some of the health food they had eaten at the sanitarium. As more orders came in through the mail, Dr. John decided to start a separate manufacturing operation, which he called the Sanitas Food Company.

Word soon spread about the tasty toasted flakes and in no time, forty-two companies sprang up in Battle Creek, all making cereal foods for the general public. Will knew it was time to escape the dominance of his brother and strike out on his own.

Will Keith Kellogg was the seventh son of a seventh son, born on the seventh day of the seventh month. The name *Kellogg* had seven letters. And it was the teachings of the Seventh-Day Adventist Church that inadvertently led him to become a leader in the breakfast food industry. He knew there had to be some significance in all of this.

W. K. Kellogg launched the Battle Creek Toasted Corn Flake Company in 1906, when he was forty-six years old. His brother, John, forbade him to use the Kellogg name because he didn't want his own reputation to be compromised. After lengthy legal battles, Will finally won the right to use his family name as a trademark in 1925. The familiar signature that still appears on each box of Kellogg's cereals is in Will's own handwriting.

On his own for the first time, Will Kellogg became a different person. He was the driving force of his rapidly growing company and proved to be a marketing genius.

At the age of seventy, Will started a new career: giving away his money. A foundation was set up in 1930 to "help people help themselves," and hospitals, schools, research centers, and needy children have all benefitted from Kellogg's generosity. The W. K. Kellogg Foundation is one of the ten largest philanthropic organizations in the country today, assisting more than four hundred projects on four continents every year.

★ James Lewis Kraft
(Kraft Cheese)

J. L. Kraft did not invent cheese, although his name has been closely associated with the popular dairy product for most of this century. In fact, Kraft sells more cheese today than any other company.

The first cheese factory didn't come into existence until two decades before James Kraft was born. Even then, cheese was made the same way it had been for centuries, using sour curd as the starter. Without refrigeration, cheese spoiled very quickly.

As a young man working in Ferguson's General Store in his hometown of Fort Erie, Ontario, James would watch housewives carefully smell cheese before buying. He resolved that he would find a way to improve the way cheese was made so it would stay fresh longer and have a uniform flavor.

James Lewis Kraft was the second of eleven children born to a Mennonite farmer and his wife. At sixteen, young James was given permission to leave home so he could earn money to help lower the mortgage on the family farm. He crossed the border to Buffalo, New York, and sold eggs to hotels and retail shops there.

James's first business experience made him realize that he needed more education. He signed up for a course at a business school in Buffalo, walking twelve miles a day to the school and back to the farm in Canada. To help pay his tuition, the ambitious young man swept and dusted classrooms.

At the age of eighteen, Kraft took the job at Ferguson's grocery. After saving some money, he invested in a cheese company. While he was looking after the company's Chicago branch, Kraft's partners eased him out of the business and the young man found himself stranded in the Windy City with only sixty-five dollars to his name.

Kraft put his merchandising experience to good use. He rented a horse and wagon, went to the wholesale warehouse district every morning to buy cheese, and resold it to small stores in the city.

By 1909, four of his brothers had joined him in Chicago. That year, J. L. Kraft and Brothers Company was incorporated, with James as president. In 1928, Kraft bought the Phenix Corporation and added their famous Philadelphia Brand Cream Cheese to the ever-growing product line. National Dairy Products Corporation acquired the Kraft-Phenix Cheese Corporation in 1930. Through the years, the National Dairy Products Corporation grew and developed to meet changing consumer demands, and the Kraft business grew with it. The corporation's name was changed to Kraftco Corporation in 1969 and was changed again in 1976 to Kraft, Inc. Today Kraft is part of Kraft General Goods, Inc., which is a business unit of Philip Morris Companies, Inc.

Looking back over his productive career, J. L. Kraft knew that he had accomplished his goal: to supply high-quality, low-priced, nutritious food to millions. What made him equally happy was what he was able to do with the profits from those sales—provide scholarship funds for hundreds of children through the 4-H Clubs of America, underwrite the education of many clergymen, and provide complete support of several foreign mission stations around the world.

★ James Cash Penney
(J. C. Penney)

His middle name was Cash, but the young boy from Hamilton, Missouri, grew up with very little of it. James's father was a farmer and Primitive Baptist preacher. He farmed on weekdays to provide for his family of twelve children and preached on Sunday without pay.

When James turned eight, he was told that he would have to buy his own clothes. His father wanted to teach him the value of money and self-reliance.

The young lad took his savings of $2.50 and bought a pig, fattening it up on leftovers from the family table. When the pig was of sufficient size, it was traded for twelve piglets. When summer came and the smell and noise from the growing herd became unbearable, James's father ordered them to be sold.

"But they're not ready to bring top price," James protested.

"I know," his father answered, "but we must consider the neighbors. The smell isn't fair to them."

That was how James Penney was taught the meaning of the Golden Rule: "Do unto others as you would have others do unto you." The lesson of never taking advantage of others became part of Penney's business philosophy and led him to become one of the great "merchant princes" of the twentieth century.

After James graduated from high school, his

father took him to see J. M. Hale, who owned the leading dry-goods store in town. The Christmas season was over and the merchant did not need any help, but if the young man wanted to learn the trade and make himself handy around the store, Hale would give him $25 the following Christmas. Eager to learn, James took the job. His earnings that year averaged $2.27 a month.

The following year his salary jumped to two hundred dollars and to three hundred dollars the year after that, but overwork caused his health to deteriorate. On the advice of his doctor, James moved to Colorado and was soon back in retailing. Using all of his three hundred dollars in savings, he bought a butcher shop in Longmont.

The shop's biggest customer was the local hotel. Penney was told by his meat cutter that if he wanted to keep the account, he would have to buy the hotel's chef a bottle of whiskey every week. When he refused, the hotel withdrew its business and Penney eventually lost the shop.

Undaunted, Penney went to work for Johnson and Callahan, who operated small dry-goods stores in Wyoming. The two men were impressed with the ambitious young man and offered him a partnership in a new store they were about to open in the frontier mining town of Kemmerer, Wyoming. The store was nothing more than a one-room shack away from the main business district. With his wife and infant son, Penney moved into the attic over the store.

Penney stocked his store with quality merchandise, established a "cash only" policy, offered a money-back guarantee, and clearly marked the price of each item even though bartering was still a common practice in most stores. Penney called his new business the "Golden Rule Store," because he believed that it was possible to combine a high order of ethics with good economics.

People said it couldn't be done, but the twenty-seven-year-old merchant proved them wrong. On his first day of business in April of 1902, he sold $466.59 of merchandise.

In time, James Penney was able to buy out his two partners and start his own chain of stores. In 1913, with thirty-four stores and sales totaling more than two million dollars a year, the J. C. Penney Company was incorporated.

Penney believed in treating his employees as well as he did his customers. They were called associates, not clerks, and they shared in the profits, which proved to be a good motivational factor.

By 1929, Penney's personal worth had grown to forty million dollars. Then came the stock market crash, which wiped out his fortune and left him virtually broke at the age of fifty-six. Penney became discouraged and ill and spent some time in a sanitarium.

The man who had always been so optimistic and full of life now considered himself a failure and wanted to die. One night, he underwent a spiritual crisis. In the morning, his faith and trust in God were restored and so was his will to live.

Penney started over again with money he borrowed from a three-million-dollar insurance policy. He regained a foothold in the company and was soon back as chairman of the board.

Looking back over his long and illustrious career, Penney credited his "associates" with much of his success. "All along the way they have strengthened me with their esteem," he wrote. "The desire to be worthy of them has made me a better man."

About his limited education he said: "I'm sorry that I didn't have a college education. I might have done a better job."

About one thing he was positive. "This company's success is due to the application of the Golden Rule to every individual, the public, and to all of our activities."

★ Dr. Thomas Bramwell Welch
(Welch's Grape Juice)

Even as a child, Thomas Welch had strong beliefs and was not afraid to express them. At the age of eleven, the English-born Welshman joined the Methodist Episcopal church in his hometown of Hammond, New York, near the Canadian border. Because of his deep feelings against slavery, the young man was driven out of the church. He joined the Wesleyan Methodists and, for several years, helped them get runaway slaves safely into Canada.

At nineteen, Welch became a preacher, but his vocal cords gave out after three years and he reluctantly had to give up the pulpit.

From spiritual healing, he turned next to physical healing. With a degree from Syracuse Medical College in 1852, he practiced medicine for four years, until he decided to become a dentist.

After several moves, Dr. Welch and his family came to Vineland, New Jersey, named for the many grape vineyards in the area. By this time, Welch had become a staunch supporter of the temperance movement. He was especially upset that even in his own church wine was used in the Communion service. He resolved to create a nonalcoholic grape juice that would not ferment.

Buying bushels of grapes at a time, he would experiment in his kitchen every evening trying to find a way to keep the natural sugar in grape juice from turning to alcohol. Fermentation, he knew, was caused by the tiny particles of yeast that collected in the fruit. He finally discovered that if he placed bottles of grape juice in pots of boiling water, the heat would kill the yeast.

In 1869, the first bottles of *Dr. Welch's Unfermented Wine* were ready for sale. There was very little interest from churches, however, since many felt that wine should be served during Communion. After four years with little success, the disheartened dentist abandoned his plans. It never dawned on him to offer his product to the general public as grape juice. It was his son, Charles, who started manufacturing *Welch's Grape Juice* and turned it into a thriving business.

When the Eighteenth Amendment passed in
1919, prohibiting the making or drinking of al-
coholic beverages, Welch's Grape Juice became a
favorite substitute for wine. Dr. Thomas Welch
would have found that a strange irony.

★ 11 ★
Was There Really an Aunt Jemima?

Some of the best-known "brand names" in the United States are not actual people, but fictitious characters who have become very real to the buying public. Aunt Jemima and Betty Crocker are just two examples of company trademarks of people who never existed.

Most of the brand names listed in this chapter belong to real people who had nothing to do with creating or developing the products that bear their names. For one reason or another, they allowed their names to be used. These little known individuals with very familiar names should step into the spotlight and be recognized for their contributions to the American business scene.

★ Aunt Jemima Pancake Mix

Chris Rutt was a St. Joseph, Missouri, newspaper-man who loved pancakes for breakfast, but he didn't like to prepare the batter from scratch every morning. Wouldn't it be wonderful, he thought, if someone could invent a self-rising pancake mix. All you would have to do was add water or milk to the mix and the batter would be ready for the griddle.

The idea sounded so good that Rutt decided to tackle the job himself. With two friends he began to experiment and soon came up with the right combination of ingredients: hard wheat flour, corn flour, phosphate of lime, soda, and salt.

The first mix went on sale in 1889. It was packaged in plain brown paper sacks and didn't sell well. Rutt realized that he needed a distinctive name and package design to go with his unique new product. The inspiration he needed came later that year when a vaudeville team named Baker and Farrell came to St. Joseph.

The show-stopper of their act was a rhythmic song called "Aunt Jemima." Baker performed the number dressed as a Southern "mammy" with apron and red bandanna. The picture of Southern hospitality and good cooking was just the image that Rutt wanted to project for his product.

An artist's drawing of a smiling black cook with apron and colorful bandanna was put on the new package, and sales for *Aunt Jemima's Pancake Mix* began to pick up. After a few years, Chris

Rutt sold his creation to the Davis Milling Company.

When the 1893 Chicago World's Fair was about to open, the new owners wanted to introduce their product to fairgoers. What better way than to bring their trademark to life? After a bit of searching, they found a warm, friendly African American woman by the name of Nancy Green who was working for a local family, and they hired her to impersonate Aunt Jemima.

At the fairgrounds, the company built the world's largest flour barrel. Inside, Aunt Jemima served up samples of her easy-to-make pancakes. Naturally, she became a hit at the fair and her pancake mix became the number one best-seller that it still is today, more than a century later.

Although Aunt Jemima is over a hundred years old, she looks younger today than she did when she first made her debut. Her image has been updated every twenty years to keep her modern-looking, but the company makes sure that she retains the same warm qualities that first made her appealing to the public.

★ Baby Ruth Candy Bar

Most candy lovers have grown up thinking that one of their favorite chocolate bars was named after the famous New York Yankee outfielder and home run king, Babe Ruth. After all, George Herman "Babe" Ruth was one of the most popular baseball players when the candy bar was introduced in 1921. But take a closer look at the candy wrapper. The name is "Baby" Ruth, not "Babe" Ruth.

The best-selling creation of Chicago candymaker Otto Schnering was actually named for "Baby Ruth" Cleveland, the very popular daughter of President Grover Cleveland. The name was suggested by one of Schnering's employees during a contest to find a suitable name. Most Americans today have never heard of Ruth Cleveland, but the candy bar named for her is still a favorite among chocolate lovers.

★ Barbie Doll

Barbie and her boyfriend, Ken, have been racking up phenomenal sales records since the popular teenage doll first made her appearance in 1959. Her creator was Ruth Handler, but the curvaceous doll was inspired by and named for Mrs. Handler's young daughter, Barbara.

Ruth Handler's husband, Elliot, had worked for a while as a picture framer. In 1945, he found himself with a lot of extra framing wood on his hands. The husband-and-wife team decided to make doll houses and doll furniture, and they called their new business *Mattel*. They later came out with a toy burp gun, and they made history when they agreed to sponsor Walt Disney's *Mickey Mouse Club* on television for a whole year. Until then, toy manufacturers advertised only during the Christmas season.

In 1959, Ruth Handler decided to come out with a Mattel doll, but not the infant baby variety that most doll manufacturers made. Mrs. Handler noticed that her daughter liked playing with paper dolls cut out from newspapers and books—she would spend hours dressing them up in the various outfits that came with the cutouts.

Mrs. Handler's doll would be a shapely young teenager and she would have an extensive wardrobe (which could be sold separately to bring in more money for the company). The doll, of course, would be called Barbie. A few years later, Barbie had a boyfriend, and he was named for the Handler's son, Ken.

★ Betty Crocker Cake Mixes

Betty Crocker is one of the best-known brand names of all time. Her portrait has appeared on packages of cake mixes and other food products for seventy years but, like Aunt Jemima, she never existed.

In 1921, the makers of Gold Medal flour in Minneapolis were getting thousands of letters from customers, asking for baking suggestions and recipes. The head of the company's advertising department decided that each letter should receive a personal reply and be signed by a single fictitious name. The name Betty Crocker was chosen.

Her last name honored William G. Crocker, a popular treasurer and director of the Washburn Crosby Company who had just died. Betty, it was decided, was a familiar and friendly nickname.

The spokesperson for the milling firm now had a name. All that was lacking was a signature to go on the bottom of the letters. A contest was held among the female employees of the company. The winning entry, submitted by a secretary, still appears on all Betty Crocker products.

Three years later, in 1924, the believable cooking expert made her radio debut with the very first cooking program to hit the airwaves. An actress was hired to impersonate the fictitious Betty Crocker, who was now becoming well known and respected across the country. Most of her fans believed that she was a real person, but no one knew what she looked like.

In 1936, on the fifteenth anniversary of Betty Crocker's creation, a New York artist was commissioned to paint a portrait of the famous lady. Instead of using one model, the artist gathered all the women in the company's Home Service Department and blended their features into one composite drawing.

In 1955 her portrait was updated. But instead of aging her nineteen years, they made her look younger and more modern. There have been several updates since. Betty Crocker still projects confidence and reliability, but she is now a contemporary professional woman.

★ Fanny Farmer Candy

Fannie Merritt Farmer was only a teenager when she suffered a stroke that left her paralyzed. Through courage and determination she overcame her handicap and went on to become a well-known cooking expert. In 1896, she wrote *The Boston Cooking-School Cookbook*. It is still published in a revised form as *The Fannie Farmer Cookbook*.

John Hayes was a candymaker who began a chain of stores in Canada, known as Laura Secord. In 1919, he decided to open a store in Rochester, New York, but he wanted it to have a distinctive new name. Because he admired the young girl who had fought so hard to overcome her paralysis, Hayes chose the name *Fanny Farmer* for his American store.

★ Frisbees

For more than thirty years, Americans have enjoyed playing with colorful plastic discs called *Frisbees*. What started out in 1957 as a fad has now become a permanent part of American sports and culture.

Walter Frederick Morrison, son of the man who invented the automobile sealed-beam headlight, inherited his father's inventive spirit. Combining his interest in flight and the remarkable new post–World War II substance called "plastic," young Morrison formed the modern-day flying disc. When it first appeared in stores, it was called a *Pluto Platter* because it resembled a flying saucer from outer space. But how did it get the name by which it is known today?

In the 1920s, some college students from New England started experimenting with flying discs by tossing round metal pie tins from the Frisbie Pie Company in Bridgeport, Connecticut. To warn onlookers that a spinning pie tin was heading their way, they would yell "Frisbie!"

★ Graham Crackers

Graham crackers were named for an eccentric Connecticut preacher named Sylvester Graham who traveled throughout the eastern part of the United States in the early 1800s, preaching against the evils of liquor and white bread. The health-food fanatic, who himself was sickly most of his life, believed that a diet of fruits and vegetables and coarsely ground whole wheat flour would cure all ills and lead to a long, healthy life. Graham also recommended frequent cold showers, hard mattresses, and loose clothing.

His impassioned lectures made Sylvester Graham the butt of many jokes. Ralph Waldo Emerson dubbed him "The Poet of Bran." Others referred to him as "Father Fiber" or "a nut among the crackers." With today's emphasis on oat bran and other health foods, the Reverend Sylvester Graham would have been right at home.

Despite his low-fat, high-carbohydrate, and

high-fiber diet, Graham remained a sickly man and died at the age of fifty-seven. But his name lives on in the nutritious graham cracker which has been eaten and enjoyed by generations of Americans.

★ Duncan Hines Cake Mixes

Mention the name Duncan Hines today and most people will immediately think of delicious home-made cakes covered with lots of rich icing. In the late 1930s, Duncan Hines was known as the author of *Adventures in Good Eating*, a guidebook to the best restaurants along America's highways. So many copies of the pocket-sized book were sold that every automobile in America could have had one in its glove compartment.

The Kentucky-born authority on good food traveled over fifty thousand miles a year visiting restaurants and updating his guidebook. Discriminating travelers would look for eating places that displayed the coveted sign: "Recommended by Duncan Hines."

In 1948, a man named Roy Park was about to come out with a line of cake mixes and other boxed baking products. Park knew that if he could put a trusted name like Duncan Hines on his products, he would have a winner. He offered the food expert a partnership in his company and Hines gladly accepted.

Roy Park knew he had made the right decision. After only three weeks on the store shelves,

Duncan Hines Cake Mixes had captured almost fifty percent of the national market.

★ Listerine

In today's antiseptic world of medicine, it is difficult to imagine a time when surgery was performed without sterilized instruments and when doctors operated with bare hands, wearing street clothes. In those days, a survival rate of only ten percent among surgery patients was not unusual.

In the 1860s, a British surgeon named Joseph Lister came to the conclusion that infections were caused by microorganisms in the air. He began to insist that surgical instruments be cleaned with carbolic acid and that dressings be soaked in a carbolic solution. He even went so far as to spray the air around the operating table with carbolic acid.

Although his patients began to show a higher rate of survival than other surgery patients, many physicians of his day scoffed at Dr. Lister's pleas for "antiseptic surgery." Dr. Lister's theories, however, did impress a Missouri physician named Joseph Lawrence.

Dr. Lawrence developed an antibacterial liquid and decided to call it *Listerine* in honor of the pioneer germ fighter, although it was reported at the time that Dr. Lister did not like having his name used in this way and objected to it.

At first, the product was sold only to hospitals and the medical profession. When dentists began rinsing their patients' mouths with the liquid, the "breath freshener" caught on with the general public.

From the very beginning, Listerine has been sold with a paper outer-wrap to give it a medicinal image. For ninety years, advertisements claimed that the mouthwash and gargle would "Kill Germs by Millions on Contact." In 1970, however, the makers of Listerine had to include in their advertising a disclaimer that Listerine could not prevent colds or sore throats or lessen their severity, as it had once claimed.

Controversy, it seems, has been no stranger to Joseph Lister or his name—even long after his death.

★ Dr. Pepper

There really was a Dr. Pepper and he *was* a physician, but he had nothing to do with the creation of the popular soft drink that bears his name. How a doctor in Virginia got his name on a carbonated beverage concocted in Waco, Texas, makes for a very interesting and unusual story.

In 1881, a young man named Wade Morrison was working as a pharmacist in a drugstore in Rural Retreat, Virginia. The store was owned by Dr. Charles K. Pepper.

The young pharmacist, fresh out of school, fell madly in love with his boss's attractive teenage daughter. Dr. Pepper did not care for the attachment—his daughter was too young and the young man had not established himself yet—and he managed to put an end to the romance.

Disappointed and discouraged, Wade Morrison left Virginia and moved to Texas, where he eventually became owner and manager of the Old Corner Drug Store in Waco in 1885. The popular establishment was the favorite meeting place of a steady group of customers who came to enjoy a glass of sasparilla or ginger ale and hear what was happening in town.

In addition to the latest gossip, the regulars heard all about Dr. Pepper's beautiful daughter and the romance that was nipped in the bud. The druggist still had a crush on the girl and couldn't get her out of his mind.

There is one more character in the story—Charles Alderton—who had graduated from medical school and decided to become a pharmacist instead of a doctor. In addition to filling prescriptions at the Old Corner Drug Store, Alderton also worked behind the soda fountain, mixing up soft drinks for the patrons. One particular creation—a blend of twenty-three fruit flavors—was different from anything he had tasted before, and his customers agreed.

Some of the drugstore regulars suggested calling the new drink *Dr. Pepper*, hoping that the honor might help Wade Morrison win favor with the father of his one and only love. The plan did not work, but Dr. Pepper went on to become one of the most popular soft drinks in the South. In later years, it was introduced to the rest of the country.

While Wade Morrison never did marry the

pretty Miss Pepper, the soft drink created in his drugstore won the hearts of many Americans.

★ Ralston Purina Company

William H. Danforth had just graduated from Washington University, and he was looking for a good business to start in St. Louis, Missouri. The year was 1893 and the country still traveled on bicycles and horseback. Every year, thousands of horses died from colic caused by bad corn. Danforth decided there was a need for an animal feed that was pure and wholesome. To emphasize purity, he named his new product *Purina*.

When Danforth found a miller who had discovered a way to prevent whole wheat from turning rancid, he added a product for human consumption, which he called *Purina Whole Wheat Cereal*.

People didn't know much about nutrition in the closing days of the nineteenth century. The word "vitamin" hadn't even been coined yet. Then Professor Albert Webster Edgerly, a law graduate of Boston University, began writing and lecturing on proper eating habits. The Ralston Health Club, which he had founded around 1897, was a worldwide organization boasting over a million members. Edgerly was so closely linked with the club that he was often called Dr. Ralston.

Danforth asked Edgerly (Dr. Ralston) to endorse his Purina Whole Wheat Cereal. Ralston agreed, if he could put his name on the product.

Because of Ralston's reputation, the newly christened cereal started selling very well. By 1902, the names of Ralston and Purina had become so closely linked that the name of the firm was changed to the *Ralston Purina Company*.

★ Sara Lee

Charles Lubin was a Chicago baker who dreamed of mass-producing a cake so rich that even the most experienced cake maker would find it difficult to duplicate. When he started his new baking company, he turned to his teenage daughter for the name. In 1951, the *Kitchens of Sara Lee* began to turn out cheesecakes, coffee cakes, and pound cakes in volume. Despite the higher prices, cake lovers knew a good thing when they tasted it and *Sara Lee* cakes have been best-sellers ever since.

★ Vicks VapoRub

Most druggists today fill prescriptions by merely counting out pills and capsules that have been manufactured in large pharmaceutical laboratories. At the turn of the century, however, pharmacists often invented their own medicines, pills, and even concocted exotic mixtures to use as tonics.

Lunsford Richardson was a druggist from Selma, North Carolina, who was looking for a treatment for chest and head colds—an ointment that would give off vapors but would not burn like scalding steam or irritate the skin.

Richardson combined the popular new petroleum jelly developed by Robert Chesebrough (Chapter 6) with another new discovery—menthol, an extract from oil of peppermint. When applied to the chest and forehead, the pungent rub opened blocked air passages while it stimulated blood circulation through skin contact.

Although Richardson couldn't work fast enough to fill orders from cold sufferers and other druggists, he knew that he needed a better name than "Richardson's Croup and Pneumonia Cure Salve." The enterprising pharmacist thought of his brother-in-law, Joshua Vick, a physician in whose laboratory Richardson had developed his ointment. The catchy name Richardson coined—*Vick's VapoRub*—is still well known today.

★ Wendy's Hamburgers

R. David Thomas owned a Kentucky Fried Chicken franchise in 1969 when he decided to switch to hamburgers and start his own restaurant. Just as Sara Lee's father had done some eighteen years before, Thomas used his eight-year-old daughter's nickname for the name of his new restaurant and a drawing of his little girl to decorate the sign.

Although Melinda Lou ("Wendy") Thomas is now a grown woman, that freckle-faced, pigtailed girl still smiles down from more than two thousand *Wendy's* restaurants today.

INDEX

About the Author

FRANK H. OLSEN is a free-lance writer who has worked in the fields of television broadcasting and advertising. He has directed and produced several films and is currently writing a video series for young children. This is his first young adult book.